Dwight D. Eisenhower

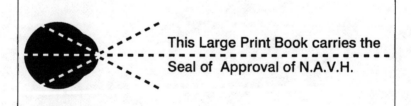

This Large Print Book carries the
Seal of Approval of N.A.V.H.

Dwight D. Eisenhower

The American Presidents

Tom Wicker

Thorndike Press • Waterville, Maine

Published in 2003 by arrangement with Henry Holt and Company, LLC.

Thorndike Press® Large Print Senior Lifestyles Series.

The tree indicium is a trademark of Thorndike Press.

The text of this Large Print edition is unabridged.
Other aspects of the book may vary from the original edition.

Set in 16 pt. Plantin by Warren S. Doersam.

Printed in the United States on permanent paper.

Library of Congress Cataloging-in-Publication Data

Wicker, Tom.
    Dwight D. Eisenhower / Tom Wicker.
      p. cm.
    Originally published: New York : Times Books, 2002.
    Includes bibliographical references.
    ISBN 0-7862-5165-4 (lg. print : hc : alk. paper)
    1. Eisenhower, Dwight D. (Dwight David), 1890–1969.
2. Presidents — United States — Biography. 3. United States — Politics and government — 1953–1961. 4. Large type books. I. Title.
E836.W53 2003
973.921′092—dc21
   [B]   2003040650

TO
JAMES RESTON
AND
WALLACE CARROLL

Editor's Note

The American Presidency

The president is the central player in the American political order. That would seem to contradict the intentions of the Founding Fathers. Remembering the horrid example of the British monarchy, they invented a separation of powers in order, as Justice Brandeis later put it, "to preclude the exercise of arbitrary power." Accordingly, they divided the government into three allegedly equal and coordinate branches — the executive, the legislative, and the judiciary.

But a system based on the tripartite separation of powers has an inherent tendency toward inertia and stalemate. One of the three branches must take the initiative if the system is to move. The executive branch alone is structurally capable of taking that initiative. The Founders must have sensed this when they accepted Alexander Hamilton's proposition in the Seventieth Federalist that "energy in the executive is a leading character in the definition of good government." They thus envisaged a strong president — but within an equally strong system of constitutional accountability. (The term *imperial presidency* arose in the 1970s to describe the situation when the balance between power and accountability is upset in favor of the executive.)

The American system of self-government thus comes to focus in the presidency — "the vital place of action in the system," as Woodrow Wilson put it. Henry Adams, himself the great-grandson and grandson of presidents as well as the most brilliant of American historians, said that the American president "resembles the commander of a ship at sea. He must have a helm to grasp, a course to steer, a port to seek." The men in the White House (thus far only men, alas) in steering their chosen courses have shaped our destiny as a nation.

Biography offers an easy education in American history, rendering the past more human, more vivid, more intimate, more accessible, more connected to ourselves. Biography reminds us that presidents are not supermen. They are human beings too, worrying about decisions, attending to wives and children, juggling balls in the air, and putting on their pants one leg at a time. Indeed, as Emerson contended, "There is properly no history; only biography."

Presidents serve us as inspirations, and they also serve us as warnings. They provide bad examples as well as good. The nation, the Supreme Court has said, has "no right to expect that it will always have wise and humane rulers, sincerely attached to the principles of the Constitution. Wicked men, ambitious of power, with hatred of liberty and contempt of law, may fill the place once occupied by Washington and Lincoln."

The men in the White House express the ideal and the values, the frailties and the flaws, of the voters who send them there. It is altogether natural that we should want to know more about the virtues and the vices of the fellows we have elected to govern us. As we know more about them, we will know more about ourselves. The French political philosopher Joseph de Maistre said, "Every nation has the government it deserves."

At the start of the twenty-first century, forty-two men have made it to the Oval Office. (George W. Bush is counted our forty-third president, because Grover

Cleveland, who served nonconsecutive terms, is counted twice.) Of the parade of presidents, a dozen or so lead the polls periodically conducted by historians and political scientists. What makes a great president?

Great presidents possess, or are possessed by, a vision of an ideal America. Their passion, as they grasp the helm, is to set the ship of state on the right course toward the port they seek. Great presidents also have a deep psychic connection with the needs, anxieties, dreams of people. "I do not believe," said Wilson, "that any man can lead who does not act . . . under the impulse of a profound sympathy with those whom he leads — a sympathy which is insight — an insight which is of the heart rather than of the intellect."

"All of our great presidents," said Franklin D. Roosevelt, "were leaders of thought at a time when certain ideas in the life of the nation had to be clarified." So Washington incarnated the idea of federal union, Jefferson and Jackson the idea of democracy, Lincoln union and freedom, Cleveland rugged honesty. Theodore Roosevelt and Wilson, said FDR, were both "moral leaders, each in his own way and his own time, who used the presidency as a pulpit."

To succeed, presidents must not only have a port to seek but they must convince Congress and the electorate that it is a port worth seeking. Politics in a democracy is ultimately an educational process, an adventure in persuasion and consent. Every president stands in Theodore Roosevelt's bully pulpit.

The greatest presidents in the scholars' rankings, Washington, Lincoln, and Franklin Roosevelt, were leaders who confronted and overcame the republic's greatest crises. Crisis widens presidential opportunities for bold and imaginative action. But it does not guarantee presidential greatness. The crisis of secession did not spur Buchanan or the crisis of depression spur Hoover to creative leadership. Their inadequacies in the face of crisis allowed Lincoln and the second Roosevelt to show the difference individuals make to history. Still, even in the absence of first-order crisis, forceful and persuasive presidents — Jackson, Theodore Roosevelt, Ronald Reagan — are able to impose their own priorities on the country.

The diverse drama of the presidency offers a fascinating set of tales. Biographies of American presidents constitute a chron-

icle of wisdom and folly, nobility and pettiness, courage and cunning, forthrightness
and deceit, quarrel and consensus. The
turmoil perennially swirling around the
White House illuminates the heart of the
American democracy.

It is the aim of the American Presidents
series to present the grand panorama of
our chief executives in volumes compact
enough for the busy reader, lucid enough
for the student, authoritative enough for
the scholar. Each volume offers a distilla-
tion of character and career. I hope that
these lives will give readers some understanding of the pitfalls and potentialities of
the presidency and also of the responsibilities of citizenship. Truman's famous sign
— "The buck stops here" — tells only half
the story. Citizens cannot escape the ultimate responsibility. It is in the voting
booth, not on the presidential desk, that
the buck finally stops.

— Arthur M. Schlesinger, Jr.

One

In the autumn of 1956, Dwight D. Eisenhower was campaigning for a second term as president of the United States. I was "Sunday editor" of the Winston-Salem, North Carolina, *Journal*, and a devout supporter of Eisenhower's Democratic opponent, Adlai E. Stevenson of Illinois. Momentarily abandoning journalistic impartiality, I raised a little money among my colleagues (the munificent sum of $150, as I recall) for the eloquent Stevenson. In those days, the *Journal* staff regarded itself as something of a family. In that spirit, Mrs. Bill Hoyt, the wife of the publisher, chided me gently about my small and no doubt improper effort.

"But Mrs. Hoyt, don't you realize," I replied in self-defense, "that Eisenhower has had a heart attack?"

Mrs. Hoyt drew herself up — she was a lady who could draw herself up impressively: "Young man," she said, "I would vote for Eisenhower if he were *dead!*"

13

She and hosts of other Americans might have done just that in 1956, because Eisenhower — known familiarly to everyone as "Ike" — was a popular incumbent revered as the victorious commander of Allied forces in the European theater during World War II and as a "man of peace" — the indispensable leader who in four years in the White House had kept the Cold War with the Soviet Union from turning hot and atomic. Throughout his tenure (1953 to 1961), as it turned out, Eisenhower was one of the best-loved presidents of the century, with an average 64 percent Gallup poll approval rating over the eight years of his two terms.

Eisenhower was, observers agreed, a "father figure" to the American voters of the prosperous and relatively tranquil fifties, many of whom had served under him in the European theater and — like good old Ike — were amateur golfers, backyard cooks, and going bald. A vast majority apparently believed that Eisenhower alone had protected them from the Russian bear and produced the rising material prosperity that had followed depression and war.

Therefore, despite his health problems

and my fund-raising, he defeated Stevenson a second time in 1956 and by an even greater margin than in 1952. Many poll-takers and politicians believe that Eisenhower could have been elected to a *third* term in 1960, had he sought it — but he couldn't, because by then the Twenty-second Amendment to the Constitution limited all presidents to two terms. Thus, ironically, a highly popular Republican was the first president turned out of the White House by an amendment that originated in the Republican Eighty-second Congress as partisan, posthumous revenge against a hated Democrat, Franklin D. Roosevelt, and his four terms.

In the eight years Dwight Eisenhower was constitutionally permitted to serve as president, the public — like Mrs. Hoyt — did not seem to mind that he spent much of his time playing golf and bridge, that his closest friends were wealthy businessmen whose frequent largesse he happily accepted, and that his health was suspect — he suffered a heart attack during his first term, a small stroke, and a bout of ileitis in his second. In the fifties, liberals and many Democrats derided him as a "caretaker" president rather than a strong chief executive in the White House, a judgment he may have encouraged but that has been considerably moderated in recent years. Most voters obviously liked things Ike's way. Times were good, after all, and the national father figure surely would keep the Soviets at bay and the economy rolling.

A self-proclaimed nonpolitician, Eisenhower was strongly conservative in domestic affairs and a convinced internationalist in foreign relations — though a hard-line anti-Communist. Nevertheless, his administration preserved much of FDR's and Truman's New and Fair Deals, though the conservative Eisenhower was contemptuous of both. He believed, however, as he told his press secretary, James C. Hagerty, "This party of ours and our program will not appeal to the American people unless [they] believe that we have a liberal program. Our hidebound reactionaries won't get to first base."[1] Eisenhower's almost constant conflict in foreign policy with those "hidebound reactionaries" gave him and his supporters the label "modern Republicans" and served to disguise the president's more palatable form of conservatism on domestic matters.

Eisenhower avoided direct personal involvement in the two great moral issues of 1950s America, school desegregation and McCarthyism — though in the latter case his admirers claim that his deliberately above-the-battle stance was an effective opposition tactic. Standing aloof, in both cases, may have guarded and even extended his popularity — but at the expense of opportunities to provide moral leadership to a nation badly in need of it.

The man of peace, moreover, fumbled in 1959 perhaps the best chance then or since for a comprehensive nuclear test ban agreement with the Soviet Union or its successor state. And the policies of the strong anti-Communist who kept the Soviets at bay and the Cold War from heating up nevertheless planted the seeds of some future troubles, including the war in Vietnam. While in office, Eisenhower feared and resisted any such combat involvement in Asia ("I don't see any reason for American ground troops to be committed in Indochina," he told Hagerty during the "French war" in 1954).[2] After his return to private life, however, he strongly backed the American war in Vietnam, because he thought a former president should support a current president and believed that if U.S. armed forces ever were committed, it was necessary for them to be successful.

Eisenhower's great political strength as president was his dedication to middle-of-the-road policies, and his insistence that he was guided only by devotion to duty and a sense of the national interest. These claims were the more believable owing to patriotic admiration for his role in World War II — still, in the decade of the fifties, the most dramatic and formative experience of many Americans' lives — and by the fact that Eisenhower had spent most of his early life in the small and ill-financed prewar army, scarcely a career to be chosen by a politically ambitious man or by one whose goals were money and power.

Dwight David Eisenhower was born in Denison, Texas, on October 14, 1890, but his father moved the family to Abilene, Kansas, a year later. There Ike, as he was already called, had a late-nineteenth-century, Tom Sawyer–like upbringing — save for the absence of the river and of Huck Finn.

One of six brothers, Dwight was raised in a white frame house on South East Fourth Street, absorbing the simple and unquestioned values taught by his surroundings and by his parents — honesty, self-reliance, hard work, ambition, and fear of God. His father, a creamery worker, read the Bible aloud to his family, and both parents preached "getting ahead." Introspection and reflection, however, were not particularly appreciated on South East Fourth nor in Abilene; and there was little racial and political diversity in a town in which virtually everyone was white, Republican, Christian, and of European descent.

"Little Ike" — brother Edgar Eisenhower was known as "Big Ike" — competed and sometimes fought with his brothers and other boys, excelled in sports, and displayed a ferocious temper — which, later in life, the army officer and president controlled but never banished. He received decent grades in school, discovered an early interest in military history, and displayed leadership qualities in organizing athletic and other outdoor events — becoming as a youngster what he remained for life, an able cook on camping trips.

In 1910, he formed a friendship with Everett "Swede" Hazlitt — who became a lifelong correspondent — an Abilene contemporary who was planning to take the 1911 service academy exam, hoping to be accepted at Annapolis. Little Ike took the service exam, too, and scored well enough to qualify for appointment to the military academy at West Point.

There, after his entrance in 1911, Dwight Eisenhower was part of another disciplined and narrow community, where questions about its values were not encouraged or even tolerated. His course of study was basically engineering, and the approved classroom method was learning and reciting by rote. None of this was intellectually or socially broadening, but his Class of 1915 (sometimes called "the class the stars fell on") was outstanding, numbering among its 164 members sixty-four young men who would become generals — and two, Omar Bradley and Eisenhower, who would earn four stars.

He performed well enough in class, gathered quite a few demerits for disciplinary offenses, and, as a yearling (which is what West Point calls sophomores) showed signs that he was about to become a star running back on the football team. A knee injury cut short his gridiron career, whereupon he became such a keen student of the game that he was asked to coach the junior varsity. A turn as a cheerleader gave him valuable experience in public appearances.

Graduation into the peacetime army, however, did not offer much to an ambitious young man. Eisenhower missed combat in World War I, but in its final stages, having done well in all his assignments, attained the temporary rank of lieutenant colonel. From there, for two decades, it was mostly downhill: back to major in 1920, to captain in 1922, up to major again in 1924, and then a twelve-year wait before he was returned in 1936 to his 1918 rank — and then mostly because all members of the Class of '15 were promoted.

Along the way, Eisenhower had married well — to Mamie Doud of Denver, who proved an ideal army and later presidential wife, managing for the couple a well-ordered household and a happy personal life, rarely interfering in her husband's career. They lost a firstborn son, a devastating blow to both, but a second son, John, was born in 1922; and in army circles, at least, Eisenhower prospered — though that was not reflected in promotion.

In 1926, Eisenhower finished first in his class at the Command and General Staff Training School in Leavenworth, Kansas, a real distinction (but his friend George Patton, a previous C&GS grad, warned him to start thinking "about making the infantry move under fire"). Later, at the War Department in Washington, he drafted a much-praised history of the army in France in World War I for Army Chief of Staff General John J. Pershing — who then sent him to the Army War College, and next to France to expand the war history by firsthand observation. When Eisenhower returned to the United States, he became an aide to Douglas MacArthur, who had succeeded Pershing as chief of staff — entering a decade in which he was to work closely with MacArthur, in Washington and the Philippines.

In these years, Eisenhower was not only good at his work, he made influential friends. He had so impressed General Fox Connor, his commanding officer in the Canal Zone — who encouraged him to read, study, and develop his intellectual capacities — that Connor had exerted his influence to get his young protégé assigned to the C&GS school. The attraction was mutual; Connor, Eisenhower said as late as 1964, was "the ablest man I ever knew," and he once conceded that "in a lifetime of association with great and good men he is the one figure to whom I owe an incalculable debt."

There were, however, a number of

others. Eisenhower learned much about administration from the difficult, politically minded MacArthur, and aped him in his mastery of details and his stubbornness in debate. From MacArthur's unfortunate example, however, Ike was confirmed in his determination to keep out of politics. Nevertheless, the controversial, publicity-minded MacArthur labeled his aide "the best soldier in the Army."

Thus, at a time when most mid-rank army officers were as unsung as worker ants, Dwight Eisenhower had attracted the favorable attention of three of the army's stars — Connor, Pershing, and MacArthur. When his assignment to MacArthur's staff and his years in the Philippines came to an end, Eisenhower spent some time in the field, notably as chief of staff of the Third Army in the great Louisiana "maneuvers" held just before World War II. But within days of Pearl Harbor, another chief of staff, George C. Marshall, summoned him to Washington; and within months Eisenhower found himself chief of the War Plans Division — and again under the wing of an important general whose greatest gift may have been his ability to judge talent.

Eisenhower's meteoric ascent within the

army in the first months of World War II, not to mention his steady accumulation, in the 'tween-war years, of jobs well done and favorable fitness reports, has to be ranked as the most impressive phase of his career — even more so than his later rise to the presidency (which, after all, depended not a little on his World War II fame and on the efforts of others). Ike's manifest abilities and Marshall's good opinion caused the chief of staff to send him to London as chief of the European theater of operations. There the modest small-town boy from Kansas with the infectious grin and the easygoing manner made instant friends with most British officials, including Winston Churchill (but not Generals Alan Brooke and Bernard Montgomery).

So he was well positioned to be given command of Operation Torch — the invasion of North Africa — when President Roosevelt reluctantly acceded to Churchill's insistence that Torch should take place before a cross-channel invasion of Europe. Eisenhower hated that decision, but command of Torch was beyond anything of which the unknown young officer of a few months earlier could have dreamed. It led on to command of the invasion of Europe — and ultimately to a great political career capped by the presidency of the United States.

Though some of Eisenhower's subordinates — notably the British general Montgomery but even the Americans Omar Bradley (his classmate) and George Patton (his old friend) — could be critical of his strictly military qualities, there was no denying that he got the job done, first in North Africa, then in Europe. All agreed that he was a superb commander, perhaps the best in history, of allied forces — a position demanding tolerance and patience with ambitious subordinates from different countries, skilled diplomacy in reacting to the sometimes imperious ways of FDR, Churchill, Charles de Gaulle, and Joseph Stalin, and masterly management of the conflicting interests of wartime allies. Such a performance demanded character and ability, and Eisenhower's ability and character obviously were of presidential potential.

To the American public after the war was won, he was simply the conqueror of Hitler, the man who had brought victory in World War II — a typical American who had risen to a demanding occasion by hard work and high merit. So it was not surprising that, in a tradition dating back to George Washington, Andrew Jackson, Zachary Taylor, and U. S. Grant, the new war hero, in whom still could be detected the modest Kansas farmboy, was quickly touted for the White House. Both Republicans and Democrats wanted him at the top of their tickets.

As the army's postwar chief of staff, Eisenhower turned down both parties for 1948, though President Truman (who denied doing so) may have offered to step down and run as the Democratic vice presidential candidate if the general would accept the party's presidential nomination.[3] In later postwar years, Eisenhower was president of Columbia University, the best-selling author of a World War II memoir, *Crusade in Europe*, and the first SACEUR (Supreme Allied Commander, Europe), assigned by Truman the task of building up and leading the armed forces of the newly formed North Atlantic Treaty Organization.

Few men have had such extensive experience in high office and international affairs. Eisenhower, by common consent, had handled all his responsibilities superbly — though at Columbia, some of the faculty regarded him as uninterested in scholarship and bored with paperwork. Still sought by both parties as their presidential candidate for 1952 and consistently a leader in national preference polls, the general with the broad grin maintained the appearance of a nonpolitician not eager, even reluctant, to run for president. This attitude was at least partially sincere, as Eisenhower often had expressed a desire to return to private life and a soldier's abhorrence of politics.

It's a question not easily answered, however, whether as 1952 approached Eisenhower clandestinely courted the Republican presidential nomination or stubbornly sought to avoid it; in seeming to do the latter he may well have cleverly done the former. He never issued a "Sherman" — a flat refusal to run or serve — but held out against a candidacy until 1952, when it was almost too late. As early as 1943, his old army and personal friend, George Patton, had remarked that "Ike wants to be president so badly you can taste it," but Eisenhower apparently believed, as 1952 neared, that he could be drafted without actually fighting for the nomination.[4]

His political views, unexceptional and shared by millions of voters, were quintessentially Republican, midwestern, middle-of-the-road, patriotic, opposed to the dependence on the state he thought was fostered by the New and Fair Deals, and suspicious of Democratic "extremes." He disliked labels like "liberal" and "conservative" though calling himself a "liberal Republican."

In international affairs, Eisenhower was an early and devout supporter of the United Nations, to the point of favoring UN control of atomic weapons. But postwar Soviet actions in Poland, Germany, Greece, and in the UN Security Council, in defiance of the Yalta agreements, slowly diminished Eisenhower's hopes for an amicable world. By late 1947, Soviet intransigence and hostility had made Eisenhower a Cold Warrior; to his diary he confessed a fear of a "battle to extinction" between the United States and "their damnable philosophy."

"Nonpolitician" or not, the general's life-long service at all levels in the army, at the head of the Allied war machine in Europe, among imperious national leaders, then in the Pentagon and at NATO, and even his years at Columbia — all situations in which political maneuverings were constant — had made him extraordinarily skilled at "personal" if not party politics.

"What the hell are you talking about?" he retorted to Merriman Smith, when in a post-presidential interview the veteran United Press International reporter said he believed Eisenhower did not like the role of politician. "I have been in politics, the most active sort of politics, most of my adult life. There's no more active political organization in the world than the armed services of the U.S."

Eisenhower's political agility was evident as he dexterously evaded, without definitively refusing, the many postwar pressures brought on him to seek the White House. In 1952, however — or perhaps when he sensed that the timing was right — he finally heeded the urgings of a group of influential Republican supporters and fund-raisers, returned to the United States from his NATO assignment, and went to his hometown, Abilene, to announce formally that, after all, he would be a candidate for that year's Republican presidential nomination.

With his wide grin, worldwide fame, outstanding record, easygoing manner, and arms extended in the familiar V-for-Victory gesture, the war hero — whether in informal groups or speaking to huge crowds — proved a splendid, though inexperienced, campaigner, with what was perhaps history's most effective political slogan: "I Like Ike."[5] The American people certainly did. Arthur Burns, then a university economist, saw the general passing in a parade and pronounced him "absolutely a natural for the presidency."[6] Burns himself was to become the first chairman of the Eisenhower Council of Economic Advisers.

In the 1952 New Hampshire primary, personal appeal, unmatched experience, and his wartime glory had enabled Eisenhower, as an unannounced write-in candidate, to defeat the Republican front-runner, Senator Robert A. Taft of Ohio, then to poll more than 100,000 votes in another test in Minnesota, whose "favorite son" candidate was former governor Harold Stassen. But in the fifties, few delegates were chosen in primaries. Taft was the champion of the conservative wing of the Republican Party ("blind, stupid isolationists," as Eisenhower later called its members).[7] He was also a veteran politician greatly admired by fellow Republicans and proved a formidable opponent, with a substantial lead in delegate strength.

Early in 1952, Herbert Brownell, who

already had managed two Republican presidential campaigns — though each was lost by Thomas E. Dewey of New York — had visited NATO headquarters in Paris and disabused Eisenhower of the unrealistic notion that he could be drafted without a contest. Brownell pointed out to the SACEUR that Taft already could count on 40 percent of the convention delegates who, in fact, would choose the Republican presidential nominee.

Eisenhower then told Brownell that he'd once met with Taft and assured him that he, Eisenhower, would not run for president in 1952 if Taft would support the internationalist view of NATO and the protection of Western Europe. Taft replied that, "in good conscience," he couldn't make such a deal.[8] Eisenhower apparently did not know that as Taft left that meeting at the Pentagon, he told companions, "By God, that's a man."[9]

The Taft-Eisenhower battle quickly became more than personal — it was also an isolationist-internationalist showdown, involving high stakes and intense emotion. Ultimately, that summer of 1952, with Taft still in the numerical lead (530 delegates to 427, the Associated Press calculated), the struggle went to the floor of the Repub-

lican National Convention in Chicago —
one of the first to be seen by millions of
Americans watching the newly developed
television networks. Among other dramatic
moments, they saw Everett Dirksen of Illinois, second only to Taft in the hearts of
the so-called Old Guard, point a long
finger at Dewey, the losing presidential
candidate of 1944 and 1948 but one of the
architects of the Eisenhower campaign,
and voice the frustration of Taft's fol-
lowers:

"We followed you before and you took
us down the path to defeat. Don't do it to
us again!"

All the fervor was not confined to the
Taftites, however. Senator Henry Cabot
Lodge of Massachusetts, who probably
would have been Eisenhower's campaign
manager had he not been preoccupied with
his own reelection effort against a young
newcomer, John F. Kennedy, remarked
later: "If Taft had won, our boys would
have walked out."[10]

Eisenhower narrowly won, however, on
the first ballot — a result that did not
reflect the closeness or the bitterness of the
contest. His nomination was owed less to
Stassen, who clinched it by switching his
delegates at the end of that first ballot,

than to the so-called fair-play amendment developed by Brownell, who consistently outmaneuvered the Taft forces at Chicago.[11]

The convention was one of the last actually to be contested rather than choreographed for television. The general-turned-candidate amply demonstrated his personal appeal and his command ability — but also a certain naïveté. He allowed a group of Republicans headed by Dewey to choose his vice presidential running mate: the youthful Senator Richard M. Nixon of California. Nixon was a double asset — a renowned Communist hunter but also, in the Dewey group's view, a bridge between Eisenhower and Taft's Old Guard.

With the naïveté went an instinctive grasp of high political strategy. Eisenhower may not have known that he could choose his own running mate but he well understood — perhaps as a former commander of Allied forces — that his candidacy would need the support of Taft and the Old Guard if Republicans were to win back the presidency that for twenty years had been held by Roosevelt and Truman. And beyond getting elected, he would need a united party if he were to lead a successful administration.

Almost as soon as his victory was certain, therefore, Eisenhower overruled tradition-bound advisers and personally called on Taft to tell him: "I hope we can work together." Next, he swallowed hard and accepted an Old Guard platform — its foreign-policy plank written by John Foster Dulles — that denounced Truman's "containment" policy and promised the liberation of Eastern Europe, a promise Eisenhower believed could not be kept without igniting a third world war. He insisted, however, on endorsement of NATO, and the platform included a halfhearted statement to that effect, along with strong condemnation of the Yalta agreements and the charge that the Democrats had "shielded traitors" in government. Watching from the White House, Eisenhower's former patron, Harry Truman, was not amused.

The platform price was high but Eisenhower paid it, thus going to work immediately to build the tenuous party unity that was barely and only sometimes to uphold his administration. For if Herbert Brownell, who was to become attorney general, had managed briefly to overcome the Old Guard–"modern Republican" split at the Chicago convention, that division would continue to afflict the party, administration, and Eisenhower, even after Taft's untimely death in 1953.

The 1952 presidential campaign was close, hard-fought, and memorable for at least three events, though its outcome was seldom in real doubt. Stevenson's eloquence and wit far outshone Eisenhower's relatively pedestrian utterances, but a mere governor of Illinois had little chance against a famous war hero and a renowned international statesman. The Truman administration and the president himself, moreover, were at a low ebb of popularity, and the Democrats had been too long in office. The nation was racked by frequent strikes and torn by what Democrats denounced as "Communist witch-hunts" and Republicans called the determined pursuit of subversives in government.

Democratic hopes nevertheless were stirred in mid-September when the *New York Post* broke a story headlined "Secret Rich Man's Trust Fund Keeps Nixon in Style Beyond His Salary." The headline was untrue in every particular but the story had a tremendous national impact at a time when Eisenhower was hammering away at "the mess in Washington" supposedly produced by numerous improprieties during the Truman administration. Many Republicans immediately assumed that Nixon was guilty; others thought that, whether or not guilty, the charge had ruined his candidacy. In either case, they concluded — and many so informed Eisenhower — that Nixon should be dropped; Dewey advised Nixon to resign from the ticket. But Eisenhower, reserving decision, told Sherman Adams, probably correctly, that "if Nixon has to go, we cannot win."

Eventually, Nixon cleared himself at least with Eisenhower (who had kept him more or less on trial for several days) with a masterly political monologue televised nationally to the biggest TV audience until then measured. This performance was remembered ever after as the "Checkers speech," owing to Nixon's mention of his children's dog, Checkers. Derided by many for its sentimentality and unction, praised by others for its candor, the speech saved Nixon's spot on the ticket (Eisenhower later told him, "You're my boy," perhaps defining the older man's view of their relationship). Quite possibly, Eisenhower's patience and Nixon's performance — a political ten-strike in 1952 — also saved the ticket itself. Public memories of the undeniably maudlin Checkers speech, however, became ever more derisive, a perception that was to plague Nixon until his death in 1994.

The stresses of the episode also shadowed relations between president and vice president throughout the subsequent eight years in Washington. At one point in his ordeal, Nixon bluntly told the war hero–candidate to "shit or get off the pot"; and in his televised speech, to Eisenhower's visible discomfort, he called on any man "who's to be president" to disclose his entire financial history, as Nixon himself had just done.

As the campaign continued, however, all seemed to be going well again for the Republicans. But when Eisenhower's campaign train rolled into Wisconsin — where in Milwaukee on October 3, 1952, he was scheduled to speak — a potentially explosive issue was also on board. Wisconsin's Republican junior senator, Joseph R. McCarthy, who had displaced Nixon as the nation's most famous Red-hunter and was running for reelection, had called Eisenhower's great benefactor, General George C. Marshall, a "traitor." Arthur Hays Sulzberger, publisher of the *New York Times* and a strong Eisenhower backer, had written a statement in defense of Marshall that Eisenhower had agreed to include in the Milwaukee speech.

As the train approached that city, Senator William Knowland of California and Governor Walter Kohler of Wisconsin, fervent McCarthy fans, discovered the proposed Marshall defense in Eisenhower's text and demanded its removal. Sherman Adams, already acting as a sort of chief of staff, told Eisenhower they regarded it as criticism of McCarthy on his home turf. Without much protest, the candidate agreed to delete the passage — an unwise, or possibly a calculated decision that he and his advisers came deeply to regret.

The deletion was discovered by William H. Laurence, a bulldog political reporter for the *Times*, who featured it the next day in his front-page story. So great was the immediate protest that the incident became the low point of Eisenhower's campaign and remains a black mark on his record. It also was the first sign of the general's reluctance — whether genuine or tactical — to tangle publicly with McCarthy, who happily shook his hand after the speech.

The failure to defend Marshall, however deplorable, was not decisive politically and the campaign continued rather routinely,

Eisenhower constantly in the lead, Stevenson attracting more admiration than support. As Election Day — November 4, 1952 — neared, Brownell dined with Emmett Hughes, then an Eisenhower speechwriter on leave from Time-Life. They agreed that public discontent with the stalemated war in Korea made it an excellent target for a well-known general to attack.

Hughes quickly turned out a speech that Eisenhower eagerly seized upon, sharpened, and delivered in Detroit on October 24. In earlier years, he had seemed to support President Truman's "police action" in Korea and also had approved Truman's decision to fire Eisenhower's old boss, General Douglas MacArthur. Now, however, Eisenhower declared that immediately after the election, he would "concentrate on the job of ending the Korean war. . . . [T]hat job requires a personal trip to Korea. I shall make that trip . . . I shall go to Korea."[12]

Ike the inexperienced campaigner had made one of the decisive strokes in American political history. He carefully had not said *what* he would do about Korea, other than to see the war for himself, thus establishing at the outset his characteristic policy of "keeping his options open." But from the hero of World War II, less than two weeks before the election, his mere pledge to "go to Korea" all but finished Stevenson and the Democrats. Even Harry Truman, the old in-fighter in the White House, could only cry "politics" — but to little avail.[13]

On November 4, 1952, the Eisenhower-Nixon ticket polled 55 percent of the popular vote and 442 electoral votes to Stevenson's 89, most of which came from what was left of the formerly "Solid South." That wasn't much, because the Republican candidates carried five southern states — Texas, Tennessee, Virginia, Florida, and Oklahoma — justifying Eisenhower's farsighted decision, against the advice of political "pros," to campaign below the Mason-Dixon line. Thus began the great modern transition of the South from a post–Civil War Democratic bastion to a post–World War II Republican stronghold.

Two

Arthur Krock has left us an admiring picture of the sixty-two-year-old Eisenhower who entered the White House on January 20, 1952. Krock was then the Washington bureau chief for the *New York Times* and a veteran observer of presidents — he had attended the 1912 Democratic convention that nominated Woodrow Wilson, and had seen them all since. As he saw Eisenhower:

> The President's stature is a happy compromise between the short and the tall. His usual complexion is ruddy under the golfing tan. His blue eyes are kindly but penetrating. His voice has the rough grain that is accepted as the token of virility, and his accent is the kind known as "Midwestern" that is prevalent in North America.
>
> His manner is genial, his ways and reflexes are kindly; his bearing is soldierly, yet his well-tailored civilian clothes never seem out of character. His smile is attractively pensive, his frequent grin

is infectious, his laughter . . . hearty. He fairly radiates "goodness," simple faith and [his] honest background.[1]

Krock was not alone in his admiration. Since George Washington, perhaps no more imposing and popular personage had taken the president's oath, to greater public expectations. And after twenty years of Democratic rule, but only two presidents, the new man and the new party seemed a welcome change.

Eisenhower, the military man of action, had not dawdled since his election, making the promised trip to Korea, beginning November 29 (though the public did not know of it until he was on the way home), choosing his cabinet in near-record time, and deciding while in Korea to seek an armistice at once.[2]

Returning to the United States aboard the cruiser *Helena*, the president-elect engaged in substantial planning for his forthcoming administration, consulting with Brownell, John Foster Dulles, and George Humphrey (the latter two already selected as the secretaries of state and Treasury). They started planning for, among other things, Eisenhower's "New

Look" in national defense.

Before and after the trip to Asia, Eisenhower had organized his administration with such unprecedented speed that by January 12, 1953, a week before his inauguration, he could hold his first cabinet meeting, at the Commodore Hotel in Manhattan. He already had his inaugural address ready, about which he said, "We want to keep . . . on a high spiritual plane . . . but at the same time [try] to relate it to our everyday living."

Not surprisingly, the cabinet members approved the speech — except that Defense Secretary-to-be Charles E. Wilson demurred briefly at a passage about trade with Communist nations; it would not be the last time Wilson's tendency to "pop off" rankled Eisenhower. The meeting proceeded to discuss the impending $10 billion budget deficit (horrendous in 1952) and to decide such momentous matters as the proper dress for the inauguration — striped ties, short coats, and homburgs.

Eisenhower had entrusted cabinet selection — reserving final decisions for himself — to two trusted associates, Brownell and Lucius Clay, and to a Taft adviser, Thomas Coleman of Wisconsin. Outvoted, Coleman soon withdrew. The only real representative of the Taft wing ultimately chosen was Ezra Taft Benson, the Mormon elder who became a dour secretary of agriculture. Clay and Brownell had a hard job, anyway, Republicans having been out of power for twenty years.

One obvious choice, Governor Dewey, removed himself from consideration. Dulles was named secretary of state first — but not before Clay and Brownell briefly considered John J. McCloy, and Eisenhower thought, also briefly, of perhaps naming Dulles to the Supreme Court. But Dulles's vast foreign policy experience apparently outweighed his fixed, sermonizing attitudes and his "dull, duller, Dulles" personality.

Never quite as modest privately as he appeared to the public, Eisenhower later told Emmett Hughes, "There's only one man I know who has seen more of the world and talked with more people and knows more than [Dulles] does — and that's me."[3] Ample evidence shows that Eisenhower, not the unimaginative Dulles, was the administration's primary decision-maker in foreign policy — as the secretary of state himself well understood.

Clay was primarily responsible for the selection of George Humphrey, a wealthy businessman who originally had been a Taft contributor but became one of Eisenhower's few close, personal friends in the government. Clay also pushed for Wilson, then the head of General Motors; that choice did not turn out so happily, owing not only to Wilson's loose tongue but to Eisenhower's special interest in and knowledge of defense matters.

The president-elect also personally assured that fixture in government, J. Edgar Hoover, that he was to remain director of the Federal Bureau of Investigation. Only one other high-level appointment was of real — though negative — significance. Governor Douglas McKay of Oregon was named secretary of the interior; neither man nor job was of first importance but the appointment originally had been offered to Governor Earl Warren of California. Warren turned it down; had he accepted he might well not have become the chief justice who personally pulled together in 1954 the Supreme Court's unanimous decision to outlaw "separate but equal" public schools.[4]

Eisenhower talked personally by telephone to Warren — Dewey's vice presidential running mate in 1948 — about the cabinet position and then told the governor, "I want you to know that I intend to offer you the first vacancy on the Supreme Court . . . that is my personal commitment to you." Neither man had any idea that the "first vacancy" would be that of chief justice.[5]

Eisenhower had demanded the inclusion in the cabinet of one woman, who turned out to be the Texas publisher Oveta Culp Hobby as secretary of the Health, Education, and Welfare Department soon to be created. With completion of the cabinet, the president-elect and his team were ready to go to work. They faced daunting challenges abroad and at home, beginning with a stalemated war in Korea and the hardening positions of the Cold War.

Eisenhower himself described — and in some cases either exaggerated or oversimplified — the world the new administration perceived. It was

caught up in a grim long-range struggle between former associated powers — the Free World on the one hand and Soviet Russia, with the now communized China, on the other. . . . [T]he world situation had continued to degenerate. Premier Mossadegh had nationalized Iran's oil resources, and the country was drifting dangerously toward Communism. In Guatemala the Arbenz regime, since December 1950, had been attempting to establish a Communist state within the Western Hemisphere. In Indochina and Malaya there was fighting between the lawfully constituted governments and the Communists. Yugoslavia and Italy were still quarreling over their claimed rights in Trieste. Furthermore, although the United States had exploded its first H-bomb on November 1, three days before the election, it was probable that the Soviets would not be far behind.

(Moscow, as the world knew, had possessed atomic weapons since 1948.)

In the United States itself, Eisenhower believed the preceding Roosevelt and Truman administrations had produced "numerous instances of malfeasance in office, disregard for fiscal responsibility, apparent governmental ignorance or apathy about the penetration of Communists in government, and a willingness to divide industrial America against itself." In his view, all this "had reduced the prestige of the United States and caused disillusionment and cynicism among our people. These I felt must be erased."[6]

A daunting world indeed, as the new administration saw it. But Dwight Eisenhower had not commanded the largest amphibious invasion in the history of warfare or organized NATO's armed forces or won an American presidential election without a high degree of self-confidence in his abilities and judgment. He was sure he could do the job, even that he was the best possible man for it, and that the country was behind him. Most Americans would have agreed — as, indeed, 55 percent of them had done on November 4, 1952.

When Dwight D. Eisenhower decided in 1952 to run for president of the United States, his highest priority was foreign policy. When he entered the White House on January 20, 1953, world affairs and the nation's role in them still were his major concerns. Eisenhower was "a man for whom the primacy of the problems of peace and war was instinctive, and for whom domestic political questions were an acquired taste."[7]

Those "acquired" tastes in 1953 did not automatically include such already-evident domestic problems as racial justice, civil liberties, and urban decay; besides, Eisenhower was eager to deal with obvious international challenges, and he had to meet a major one, with mixed success, less than two months after his inauguration. On March 3, 1953, a servant found Marshal Joseph Stalin sprawled on the dining room floor of his fortresslike dacha; the Soviet dictator died five days later. The forces on the principal sides of what Winston Churchill already had dubbed the "Iron Curtain" would be in new and untried hands.

After the usual murky maneuverings in the Kremlin (including the murder of the NKVD chief Lavrenti Beria), a new Soviet leader, Georgi Malenkov, emerged talking of "peaceful coexistence" with the West. In Washington, the rigidly anti-Communist secretary of state, John Foster Dulles, was suspicious of Malenkov's motives and doubted Malenkov would prove to be Stalin's real successor as the long-term leader of the USSR. But Churchill — back in power in Britain, though nearing senility — thought he might make progress with Malenkov and called for a more flexible approach, specifically a "summit" meeting. Dulles, fearing that the Soviets would hold up, perhaps halt, West German rearmament, counseled delay. No summit took place.

Charles E. "Chip" Bohlen, the Soviet expert whom Eisenhower had named ambassador to Moscow (over right-wing Republican objections and Dulles's hesitation), regarded this as a missed opportunity — and by 1954, when Nikita Khrushchev and a more confrontational approach took over Soviet leadership, Bohlen appeared to have been right.

In collaboration with Emmett Hughes, Eisenhower pursued his own approach. Recognizing Stalin's death as a turning point, the president told Hughes it was time for leaders on either side to "begin talking to each other." He and Hughes then crafted a speech that was delivered to newspaper editors on April 16, 1953, when the new president showed himself not altogether inhibited by Cold War rigidities.

He called for an armistice in Korea, an Austrian peace treaty, free elections to reunify Germany, and "the full independence of the East European nations," in return for an arms-limitation agreement and international control of atomic energy by the United Nations. That much was obvious propaganda — in effect, asking the Soviet Union to give up its gains from

World War II in return for little more than U.S. promises and American goodwill. But there was more.

In the present situation, Eisenhower told the editors, the "burden of arms" was "draining the wealth and labor of all peoples" because "every gun that is made, every warship launched, every rocket fired, signifies, in the final sense, a theft from those who hunger and are not fed, who are cold and are not clothed."

Then, overcoming a sudden, midspeech stomach upset, he ticked off often-ignored facts:

> The cost of one modern heavy bomber is this: a modern brick school in more than thirty cities. It is two electric power plants, each serving a town of sixty thousand population. . . . We pay for a single fighter plane with a half-million bushels of wheat. We pay for a single destroyer with new homes that could have housed more than eight thousand people. This is not a way of life at all. . . . Under the cloud of threatening war, it is humanity hanging from a cross of iron.

The United States, the president

pledged, would devote its savings from the disarmament he envisioned to a "fund for world aid and reconstruction."

That, too, may have been propaganda, and so the Soviets took it. But Eisenhower's evocation of the costs of war and preparations for war was so plain-spoken and apparently sincere — "Ike" at his midwestern best — that it struck a responsive nerve throughout the Western world as well as many neutral nations and even among some of the Soviet satellites. At home and abroad, Eisenhower's popularity soared, as did public confidence in his leadership; he seemed, indeed, to have turned a page in the Cold War by having begun talking to the other side.

Not surprisingly, however, new leadership or no, Moscow regarded Eisenhower's effort as propaganda, which was its primary consequence, and probably in the main its purpose. That Eisenhower had not really been prepared to match his powerful words with equally significant deeds was suggested by a private conversation with James Hagerty a year later. The rivalry and infighting that had marked the leadership of the Soviet Union since Stalin's death, Eisenhower told Hagerty, not only had caused Beria to be "done away with" but, by the time of the conversation, Malenkov would be out, too. The president had opposed Churchill's call for a summit conference in 1953, he said, because if at that time any Soviet leader had been able to sit alone at the table with Churchill, Eisenhower, and a French premier, that Russian would have been greatly strengthened in Soviet politics.

That, Eisenhower said, would have tended "to minimize the struggles for power that are going on within Russia. We certainly don't want to do that."[8]

Army-trained and staff-oriented as Eisenhower was, one of his first presidential moves was to revitalize — which to him meant reorganizing along military lines — the so-called National Security Council, an innovation of the Truman administration. Joseph E. Dodge, Eisenhower's budget director, and Secretary of the Treasury Humphrey were added to the NSC membership — an early indication of Eisenhower's belief that national security must rest on a strong economy. He further provided the NSC with a staff of experts, brought in a Boston banker, Robert Cutler, as a special assistant to manage that staff, and decreed weekly NSC meetings that Eisenhower himself almost always attended.

Cutler would prepare in advance a document on a particular international problem — perhaps Korea, or rearming Germany, or Latin American relations — not necessarily a "breaking news" matter but one for which advanced planning seemed prudent. That document would be circulated for study by individual NSC members; then the full council would discuss the problem in detail, Eisenhower himself often taking part in the give-and-take debate.

The majority did not necessarily rule; the president reserved the right to decide the issue — if a "decision" was in order — but only after all NSC members had been heard, and *after* the formal meeting and sometimes discussion with a smaller group in his office. Cutler would then draw up a "Record of Action," which had the force of a policy decision, and if action were stipulated, see that it was carried out.

This detailed procedure not only reflected Eisenhower's experience — his lifelong reliance, as a military man, on organized staff work and contingency planning — it also brought the order, form, and direction to foreign policy–making that the new president believed necessary.

This obviated the sort of informal and unplanned procedures that often occurred in the earlier FDR and later Kennedy and Johnson administrations. On Eisenhower's watch, when trouble popped up anywhere in the world, an NSC paper and perhaps a presidential decision probably existed somewhere in the files to guide the U.S. response.

There was a downside to this orderly procedure, and not just a loss of spontaneity. William P. Bundy, an official in the Eisenhower, Kennedy, and Johnson administrations, commented in an oral history for the LBJ Library in Austin, Texas: "I think [Johnson's] style generally carried lack of system and structure way too far. [But] I lived through the Eisenhower period when there was too much of it."

Bundy was suggesting that Eisenhower's staff procedures could enshroud "policy" in bureaucracy. On a given subject, policy could become fixed and in some cases immutable; and it seems to have been insufficiently understood that as time and circumstances changed an outmoded course of action, if approved by the president and the NSC, still might be seen as "official policy."

Thus, for instance, in 1959–1960, long

after the need for a neutral coalition government in Laos had become clear to successive U.S. ambassadors in Vientiane, all of whom made their views known in Washington, the Eisenhower administration, relying on earlier NSC decisions and the CIA's advice from previous years, clung to insistence on a pro-American, anti-Communist government. Those NSC decisions, "finalized" in Eisenhower's military staff style, had "foreseen unilateral American intervention, if necessary, to save Laos, Cambodia, or South Vietnam from Communism" and would have "committed the United States to a series of extraordinarily militant and risky policies," including the possible use of nuclear weapons in Southeast Asia.[9] These decisions, which took too little account of developing political and military realities, still were "official" doctrine when the Kennedy administration took charge of the problems of Southeast Asia in January 1961, and were to haunt its decision-makers and planners even when the NSC papers no longer were regarded as operative.

Reform of the NSC was an organizational matter, however; many other problems in 1953 required *action*. To the disappointment of the Old Guard, these did *not* include the so-called liberation of Eastern Europe — for which Eisenhower had campaigned only halfheartedly, as a sop to Dulles, the Taftite right wing, and important ethnic voting blocs. But when President Truman warned publicly that actual pursuit of "liberation" could lead to atomic war, candidate Eisenhower explained that he meant liberation "by every peaceful means, but only by peaceful means" and commanded Dulles to make the same qualification.[10] That was the death knell of "liberation" in the campaign.

The Taft wing, thus unable to pursue one favored approach, even with a Republican in the White House, turned to another: the Dulles platform's pledge to repudiate the Yalta agreements. Again, Eisenhower occasionally had denounced these during the campaign. Once in office, he found the British solidly opposed to repudiation, as were Democrats. The Soviets would have been outraged. And anyway, Western occupation rights in Berlin and Vienna had been certified at Yalta; were they to be repudiated, too?

Eisenhower met Old Guard desires with a weak congressional resolution that did not repudiate Yalta after all, but did castigate the Soviets for distorting the agreements' meaning and using them as an excuse for "subjugating whole nations." Taft tried to amend the resolution to say that it did not determine "the validity or invalidity" of the agreements; the Democrats, however, supported the original resolution unchanged; and there the matter hung until Stalin's death in March 1953 took everyone off the hook. Both sides then saw that repudiation of an act to which the late Stalin had been a vital party would be of dubious effectiveness and would callously reopen old wounds. Even Taft decided to drop repudiation; and Eisenhower was only too glad to follow his lead. What Old Guardsmen called the administration's "powder puff resolution" was allowed to languish and die.

The fortuitous intervention of the Soviet dictator's death may also have helped — at least peripherally — to solve the problem of the inherited, stalemated, highly unpopular war in Korea. Surveying the battlefront the previous November, Eisenhower had decided to seek an armistice. The soldier in him recognized, as he put it in his memoirs, that "small attacks on small hills would not win this war," while the statesman perceived that a major offensive — though advocated by MacArthur, the Pentagon, Syngman Rhee, and Dulles — probably would not have the necessary American and world support, and might bring an unwelcome response from the Soviet Union.[11]

In this situation Eisenhower supposedly threatened the North Koreans and the Chinese with atomic weapons, whereupon they hastily came to terms. In fact, Eisenhower only allowed his Communist adversaries to *fear* that he might use the A-bomb — in 1953 a reasonable apprehension he never denied. Thus, he kept his options open, as he preferred. He never issued a public and probably did not make a private threat; indeed, it's hard to see how an atomic attack would have differed — except in its greater severity — from the major offensive he did not want to launch, or why the former would not have provoked the Soviets and the latter might have.

The Chinese, however, did resume negotiations that had been dormant since late 1952, including discussion of the sticking point: forced repatriation of prisoners of war. The probability is that they acted owing to uncertainty about the intentions of the war hero in the White House (in 1953, far less inhibition on the bomb's use existed than does today; Dulles, for one, wanted the A-bomb considered a conventional weapon). Beijing appears also to have had qualms after Stalin's death about the level of support from the Soviet Union that the Chinese could expect in the future.

The talks collapsed again in mid-May, whereupon Dulles is supposed to have repeated the atomic threat to Nehru of India. If he did — his report says nothing about such a threat — it was superfluous. Two weeks *before* the Dulles-Nehru meeting, the Chinese offered important concessions on the POW issue — terms previously offered by Truman but rejected by the Communists in December 1952. After some hesitation, Eisenhower, too, adopted that formula and said — the nearest he came to an open atomic threat — that unless the Chinese settled on that basis he would pursue the war along lines not yet taken.

On July 27, despite last-ditch resistance by President Rhee of South Korea (nearly causing an exasperated Eisenhower to try to oust the old man), the armistice that had eluded Truman was formally signed.

Just six months after Eisenhower had been sworn in, the Chinese had agreed to voluntary repatriation and the new president had scored an impressive triumph.

Three

The Korean experience exerted strong influence on Eisenhower's subsequent defense and national security policies, embodied in what Dulles described as "massive retaliation." The lesson of the drawn-out "police action" in Korea and its unpopularity in the United States was that the American people did not favor fighting small wars around the world, with less than total victory in the Cold War at stake. And as early as the president-elect's return voyage from Korea aboard the *Helena* in late 1952, Admiral Arthur Radford — soon to be chairman of the Joint Chiefs of Staff — had proposed reducing American garrisons abroad in order to build up a powerful reserve of military strength in the United States, a reserve mobile enough to exert striking power anywhere in the world.

Radford's proposal comported well with one of two central ideas that Dulles had touted to Eisenhower when they had met in Europe earlier in 1952: liberation of the satellite states and swift retaliation against

Communist moves elsewhere in the world. Eisenhower, never much favorable to liberation, had liked the idea of retaliation. Dulles saw in Radford's proposed mobile reserve, with atomic weapons added to its power, a retaliatory instrument to fit his views. In the *Helena* discussions, Eisenhower accepted the ideas of both men; they suited his belief in preserving U.S. economic strength as integral to its military power.

Once in office, moreover, the new president found that even his military expertise and reputation could not persuade the Joint Chiefs to reduce the budgets of the three military services as much as he thought the overall budget demanded, unless defense policy were to place greater reliance on atomic and nuclear weapons. General Matthew B. Ridgway of the army, in particular, opposed the demanded cuts, an offense Eisenhower appears to have resented. Meanwhile, three task forces of the reorganized NSC, reviewing defense policy, risked Old Guard wrath to rule out "liberation" but opted to continue the Truman policy of "containment" of Communism. Outlined in NSC 162/2, the new defense policy would maintain offensive striking power and consider nuclear weapons as being just as "available for use as other weapons."

That was the Eisenhower "New Look," with overall costs reduced from $35 billion to $31 billion but with "more bang for the buck" — a slogan of the time — supposedly provided by increased reliance on atomic and nuclear weapons. Twenty army divisions were to be cut to fourteen by 1957, and the services were to be reduced by a half-million men — the air force being the only gainer in personnel. In January 1954, Dulles could boast to the Council on Foreign Relations, in a speech Eisenhower had approved, that the United States now would rely on "massive retaliatory power" to halt aggression "by means of our choosing."

That, of course, as the world noted and was meant to, left open the "option" of using nuclear weapons when it was considered necessary. Again, Ridgway, who thought the New Look was unbalanced, an "all or nothing" policy, was something of a holdout. With the considerable benefit of hindsight, Robert Divine observed in *Eisenhower and the Cold War* that the Republican administration, hoping to avoid small wars and to limit defense costs, actually had "opted for a policy of deterrence" instead of Truman-style containment.[1]

Meanwhile, France was losing its war in Indochina against the rebelling Viet Minh, despite the substantial American help Truman had committed in 1950 (when his primary motive was to keep France from going Communist). By 1953, the United States was paying most of the huge costs of the "French war," while having little say about its conduct. The French commander, General Henri Navarre, had made what Eisenhower in his military judgment considered the mistake of committing French forces to the supposed "fortress" of Dienbienphu — apparently in hopes of forcing the Viet Minh into a conventional war showdown. Instead, Navarre's army found itself isolated, under siege, and fighting for its life in the spring of 1954.

This produced a dilemma in Washington because the NSC had declared Indochina "vital to the security of the United States" and portrayed a negotiated settlement of the French war as tantamount to the loss of Indochina to Communism. (The nationalist Viet Minh were considered Communists in Washington and Paris, where China or the Soviet Union, or both,

65

were believed to be behind the war.) Eisenhower had no interest in helping France save what was left of its colonial empire, but he did want to keep Indochina in the so-called free world. Therefore, he repeatedly urged the French to grant independence as a war measure, in the belief that they could not win what was at least in part a colonial war. But Paris steadfastly refused any thought of granting independence.

As steadfastly, Eisenhower avoided involving the United States in a ground war in Indochina. To the NSC on January 8, 1954, he stated emphatically that he "simply could not imagine the United States putting ground forces anywhere in Southeast Asia. . . . [H]ow bitterly opposed I am to such a course of action. This war in Indochina would absorb our troops by divisions!"

On March 10, to a news conference, he was even more decisive: "There is going to be no involvement of America in a war unless it is a result of the constitutional process that is placed upon Congress to declare it. Now let us have that clear." Eisenhower well knew Congress would not declare war on behalf of the French, or even to save faraway Indochina from Communism.

Actually, indulging a taste for covert warfare that later would be well-known, Eisenhower *did* intervene in the French war, ordering the so-called Civil Air Transport — an airline secretly operated by the CIA and later renamed Air America — to help resupply French forces at Dienbienphu. CAT pilots flew 684 sorties and one pilot, James B. McGovern, was shot down on May 6 and died the next day.[2] By then, moreover, the president officially had committed the first American ground personnel to Indochina — two hundred air force technicians to service ten bombers he also had sent to the French.

At a Republican congressional leaders' meeting in February, Senator Leverett Saltonstall of Massachusetts questioned the latter commitment. The president explained — rather defensively — that he had sent fewer technicians than the French had wanted and that he fully intended to pull them out of Indochina by June 15. He also conceded that he was "frightened about getting ground forces tied up in Indochina." More passionately, he argued that he had had to do *something:* "We can't get anywhere in Asia by just sitting here in Washington and doing nothing. My God, we must not lose Asia. We've got to look the thing in the face."[3]

Eisenhower, in fact, had set conditions for open U.S. participation in the Indochinese war that he was reasonably certain could not be met: not only must France request it but Congress must approve and Britain, Australia, and New Zealand must participate.

Facing catastrophic defeat at Dienbienphu, and thus in the war, the desperate Paris government did send its army chief of staff, General Paul Ely, to Washington in a last-ditch effort to secure the desired U.S. assistance. Ely found Eisenhower still unresponsive, in the absence of positive movement by the French on Indochinese independence or ratification of the European Defense Community — a major concern for the president since his days as SACEUR. The French general did discover a willing listener in Chairman Radford of the Joint Chiefs; Radford helped work out a plan called Operation Vulture — an American air strike on Dienbienphu by 60 B-29s from the Philippines and 150 of the navy's carrier planes, possibly with a small number of atomic bombs. Intervention indeed!

Radford and Foster Dulles met with the

congressional leaders (including a future president, Lyndon B. Johnson of Texas) on April 3, 1954. The leaders made it clear that unless intervention was supported by the NATO allies, especially Great Britain, Congress would not approve direct U.S. intervention in Indochina — approval the administration would need if it were to honor Eisenhower's news conference pledge and avoid another "presidential war" less than a year after the Korean armistice. Such congressional resistance was exactly what Eisenhower wanted; he cabled Churchill to urge "united action," confident that he would be refused, and he was. Even France did not want the Indochinese war "internationalized." Eisenhower's three conditions for intervention not having been met, he then rejected Operation Vulture on April 5, 1954.

Thus, one of his most famous statements, made to a news conference two days later, probably should be seen as an effort to convince the American public of the importance of Indochina, even — or perhaps especially — if there were to be no direct American intervention in the French war. Eisenhower pointed out, first, that Southeast Asia produced vital materials; second, that the Indochinese people were being threatened, as he believed, with a dictatorial regime "inimical to the free world." But even more important, he declared, was "the 'falling domino' principle. You have a row of dominoes set up, you knock over the first one, what will happen to the last one is the certainty that it will go over very quickly."[4]

So if Indochina were lost, he was suggesting, Burma, Thailand, Malaya, even Indonesia would quickly follow — and the progression of events might even topple Japan, Formosa, and the Philippines, thus threatening Australia and New Zealand. This apocalyptic vision has been much disputed over the years, especially after the North Vietnamese conquest of South Vietnam in 1975, when the dominoes failed to topple as predicted. But in 1953, in the depths of the Cold War, from the victor of World War II, the "domino theory" had much force and a certain popular logic.

At about this time, in a letter to General Alfred Gruenther, who had succeeded him as SACEUR, Eisenhower first raised the idea of a Southeast Asia Treaty Organization, a free-world alliance to defend its signatories against Communism. He might not be willing to help the French in what he regarded as a losing and partially colonial war, but he was already thinking about the longer-term defense of Southeast Asia, against a Communist world (still considered monolithic) that he believed was determined to conquer or subvert the region.

Eisenhower's decision against intervention in April 1954 — apparently final — was challenged one more time. On April 30 or May 1, Cutler brought the president an NSC paper exploring the possibility of using atomic bombs in the Indochinese crisis. According to his own recollection, Eisenhower exploded: "You boys must be crazy. We can't use those awful things against Asians for the second time in less than ten years. My God."[5]

Dienbienphu fell, finally, on May 7, without open American intervention. Eisenhower continued to work on setting up SEATO and dealt calmly with another war scare — the belief, inspired by the French and shared by Dulles, that the Chinese were about to move into Indochina. The president told a news conference that the "preventive war" that many were calling for was "just ridiculous in itself." He warned Dulles that if the United States struck at China it might well have to attack

Russia, too, and told Chairman Radford that such an attack indeed would have to be on both Communist nations — World War III.

At a meeting of the service chiefs at Quantico, he asked them pointedly: "Gain such a [preventive war] victory and what do you do with it? Here would be a great area from Elbe to Vladivostok and down through Southeast Asia . . . torn up and destroyed . . . just an area of starvation and disaster. I ask you what would the civilized world do about it? I repeat, there is no victory except through our imaginations. . . ."[6]

The Geneva Conference was under way that summer of 1954, with the Eisenhower administration participating only unofficially. On July 21, conferees agreed to the partition of Indochina, establishing South and North Vietnam as separate national entities, but calling for elections to achieve reunification within two years. Thus, the Viet Minh, victors in war, became the losers in peace: the unified Indochina they had fought for was thwarted by international agreement — and another, future war was all but guaranteed.

Eisenhower acceded to partition but insisted, again to a news conference, that "the United States has not itself been a party to or bound by the decisions taken." By that time, moreover, the organization of SEATO was well advanced; and in September the United States, France, Britain, Australia, New Zealand, Thailand, the Philippines, and Pakistan pledged themselves to defend Southeast Asia, including Laos, Cambodia — and the new "nation" of South Vietnam.

Eisenhower had seen to it that there had been no open U.S. intervention in the French war and no "preventive" atomic or nuclear assault on China and/or the Soviet Union. Virulent anti-Communist that he was, however, he did not intend to abandon Indochina to Communism. Before the autumn ended, he had committed — fatefully — American aid to Ngo Dinh Diem, the new South Vietnamese prime minister (chosen by the CIA), "to assist . . . in developing and maintaining a strong, viable state capable of resisting attempted subversion or aggression through military means."

That future president Lyndon Johnson, who with other congressional leaders would not approve U.S. intervention in Indochina in 1954, was to insist a decade later that Eisenhower's aid commitment was justification for sending 500,000 American troops to fight "aggression" against South Vietnam.

Foreign policy in general and Southeast Asia in particular were not the only problems President Eisenhower dealt with at home and abroad in the eventful summer of 1954. Though France finally refused to ratify the European Defense Community, he pushed through arrangements for what he most wanted, German rearmament and membership in NATO. On Capitol Hill, despite his warring Republican majorities and his low priority for domestic affairs, he achieved needed tax revision, an extension of the Social Security system, and funds for U.S. participation in the Saint Lawrence Seaway. Less happily, the nation's economy went into a brief recession. A series of nuclear tests conducted by the Atomic Energy Commission on Bikini atoll in the Pacific aroused great public fear that this new power might consume its creators, or at least shower them in lethal "fallout." The Supreme Court had shaken the nation to its roots with its historic decision banning school segregation, and the president was locked in a vicious intraparty struggle with the aggressive Senator Joseph R.

McCarthy of Wisconsin.

All this was the stuff of headlines. More ominous for the long run was what the public did not yet know — that the Eisenhower administration also had precipitated two "secret wars," one winding down in Pyrrhic victory in Iran in 1953, the other intended to topple an elected, legitimate government in Guatemala. Both wars were waged by the CIA and both were fully approved by Dwight D. Eisenhower, the man of peace who had stopped a war in Korea and kept the nation out of another in Indochina.

Neither secret war, in the unblinking hindsight of history, was necessary to "stop Communism"; and both heralded a dark American record that would unfold in subsequent decades — subverting governments, supporting despots, and exerting clandestine force, all in secret, all in the name of freedom and democracy. Eisenhower's appetite for covert action, whetted by Air America's secret supply missions to Dienbienphu, cannot be held totally responsible for that record. In Indochina, Iran, and Guatemala, however, it was Dwight Eisenhower who started the nation down that slippery slope.

Just before he left office, in a written report to the president, his Board of Consultants on Foreign Intelligence Activities (which included Robert Lovett and David Bruce) advised him on January 5, 1961:

We continue to have concern as to whether the Clandestine Services of CIA are sufficiently well organized and managed to carry out covert action programs. Further, we have been unable to conclude that, on balance, all of the covert action programs undertaken by CIA up to this time have been worth the risk or the great expenditure of manpower, money and other resources involved. In addition, we believe that CIA's concentration on political, psychological and related covert action activities tended to detract substantially from the execution of its primary intelligence-gathering mission. We suggest, accordingly, that there should be a total reassessment of our covert action policies and programs.

That report was written too late for at least two governments — those of Iran and Guatemala in 1953 and 1954. And the Bay of Pigs fiasco was just a few months ahead.

So secret was U.S. activity in Iran and

Guatemala that it was years before details came to light — and some still are shielded by official government secrecy. The intervention in Iran, however, clearly was rooted in colonialist exploitation of Iranian oil. For years, that nation's ample supply of oil had been pumped, refined, and marketed by the Anglo-Iranian Oil Company, which transferred out of Iran about $2.4 billion of $3 billion in gross revenues between 1913 and 1951, while paying Iran only about 10 percent of company profits. Not surprisingly, therefore, the Iranian parliament and Prime Minister Mohammed Mossadegh — a weepy but tough old man who did most of his business from a sickbed — nationalized Anglo-Iranian in 1951.

That raised, in Washington, the dread specter of Communism — not hard to do in the early fifties, under Republican *or* Democratic administrations. After Eisenhower, the hardline anti-Communist, took office in January 1953, the new president rebuffed Prime Minister Mossadegh's request for continuation of foreign aid that had been authorized by Truman. He also joined in British planning "to bring about a change" in the Mossadegh government, approving Operation Ajax — a covert scheme jointly brainstormed by the CIA and the British Secret Intelligence Service.

The old prime minister played into the plotters' hands and confirmed their overheated fears of Communism by moving to oust the shah — Reza Pahlavi — as commander in chief of Iranian armed forces, and by opening trade talks with the Soviet Union. As prearranged with the CIA and the SIS, the Shah retaliated by dismissing Mossadegh and naming Fazollah Zahedi (a Nazi sympathizer in World War II) to replace him as prime minister. Before the public could react, Pahlavi hurriedly took off with Queen Soraya for Italy and the Caspian seacoast.

Mossadegh's supporters poured into the streets accompanied by Communist sympathizers seizing the opportunity. The CIA-SIS team (the CIA operative-in-charge was Kermit Roosevelt, the son of President Theodore Roosevelt) turned loose the estimated six thousand counter-rioters it had recruited and was holding ready. Chaos briefly ruled Tehran, so Mossadegh tried to call out the police to restore order. Again as prearranged, the Iranian military seized power instead, suppressed all demonstrations, and arrested Mossadegh.

Ajax had worked as planned, and the

Shah could come home to Iran and twenty-six years of unchecked power amounting to despotism. Eisenhower quickly restored the suspended Truman foreign aid program, increasing it from $23.4 million to $85 million; by the time he left office in 1961, he had poured nearly $1 billion into what he considered a stable anti-Communist ally — Reza Pahlavi's Iran. In August 1954, as Eisenhower and Dulles busied themselves organizing SEATO, Iranian oil production resumed — and again the Iranian people were the losers, receiving only half the revenues derived from their own oil.

There was even less excuse — save Eisenhower's strong anti-Communism — for the United States to overthrow Guatemala's elected government in 1954. In that traditionally poor Central American country, the United Fruit Company (locally known as El Pulpo, "the Octopus") ran the railways and the power company, owned 42 percent of the land, managed Puerto Barrios, the only port, paid no taxes or import duties, and had helped sink the country in poverty, repression, and feudalism.

A limited Guatemalan revolution — remarkable in the circumstances — led in

1944 to free elections; and in 1951, Jacobo Arbenz Guzman became the second elected president and undertook a land reform aimed at recapturing 178,000 acres from El Pulpo. He also planned a new electric plant and a road network, generally threatening United Fruit's dominance. By 1952, as the Red scare of the fifties began seriously to infect the United States, the Truman administration ludicrously declared Guatemala a "Russian-controlled dictatorship."

In 1953 the Eisenhower administration brought into office the Dulles brothers, Foster and Allen, who had been among United Fruit's lawyers. "Beetle" Smith, the undersecretary of state and Eisenhower's wartime chief of staff, was later to become a director of the company, as was John J. McCloy, president of the World Bank. Less than a year after Eisenhower was sworn in, Operation Success, a secret plan to "bring about a change" in Guatemala, too, was well advanced, this time involving the CIA alone.

One Carlos Castillo Armas, a former Guatemalan colonel who in 1949 had led a brief insurrection against Arbenz's predecessor, was located in exile in Honduras and recruited to lead a new revolt. A "rebel" army and air force were trained by the CIA, in Honduras; and some credence was lent to a phony Central American Red alarm when Arbenz, his efforts to buy U.S. arms rebuffed, ordered two thousand tons of munitions from Czechoslovakia. The Czechs, as it turned out, conned Arbenz, most of the weapons turning out to be virtually unusable in Guatemala.

On April 26, Eisenhower told a meeting of Republican legislative leaders that what was happening in Guatemala was "the usual Red penetration with a small minority." When that country's current foreign minister had been ambassador to the United States, Eisenhower informed the leaders, "I gave him unshirted hell but he's playing along with the Communists"; and now the Reds were trying to break out of Guatemala into other South American countries. "Where in hell," Eisenhower asked, speaking of the world in general, "can you let the Communists chip away anymore? We just can't stand it."[7]

A little later, in May 1954, Secretary Dulles conceded to Latin American ambassadors that he had no "evidence" linking Guatemala to Moscow, but insisted that "such a tie must exist" and therefore the Soviet Union "could not be allowed to establish a puppet state in this hemisphere."[8] The U.S. Information Agency flooded the Latin press with propaganda, and on June 18, 1954, Castillo struck with all the force of a fly-swatter. Riding in an old station wagon, he led an "army" of about 140 men out of Honduras and six miles into Guatemala, "covered" by his ancient "air force" — about a dozen World War II P-51s and P-47s and three old bombers.

Not least among those deceived was the *New York Times*, whose headline, "Revolt Launched in Guatemala," lent substance to CIA disinformation.[9] Even with a half-century's hindsight, it's difficult to see how a reputable newspaper and most of the world could have been fooled into believing a popular uprising actually was under way. The truth was that Castillo's invading "army," which was not remotely a product of the oppressed Guatemalan people, invaded no farther than the initial six miles; his "air force" dropped only leaflets, a hand grenade and a stick of dynamite, and lost two of its planes to ground fire. Another crash-landed in Mexico, where the CIA covered up for its American pilot.

Operation Success did not seem to be going as well as Ajax had — until

Anastasio Somoza, the dictator of Nicaragua and a U.S. puppet, offered to provide two modern fighter-bombers to support Castillo, on condition that the United States send him replacements. Eisenhower struck the deal with Somoza — he recalled in *Mandate for Change* — after Allen Dulles told him that if he didn't, Castillo's chances were "about zero." Somoza's planes, going into action on June 21 — a foreign intervention, not a people's uprising — turned things around. Castillo's radio jammed Guatemalan airwaves, claimed the "rebels" were constantly advancing, and confused Arbenz as to the real situation. On June 27, the Guatemalan president's own army — equally confused or, more likely, guided by the CIA — demanded his resignation and he quickly complied.

On July 3, Castillo landed in Guatemala City in a U.S. aircraft, accompanied by U.S. Ambassador John Peurifoy sporting a pistol in a holster. Foster Dulles could proclaim: "Now the future of Guatemala lies at the disposal of the Guatemalan people themselves."[10]

In fact, Arbenz's land reform was cancelled, unions were outlawed, hundreds of political and labor leaders were exiled, unknown numbers of *campesinos* were murdered, thousands were arrested, political parties were suspended, and three-quarters of the people were disenfranchised because they were illiterate. For years to come, Guatemala was racked by guerrilla warfare, coups and countercoups, murder and repression. Castillo Armas himself was assassinated in 1957, despite the "freedom" and the "liberation" from Communism that he and the CIA, with the approval of Dwight Eisenhower, had brought to Guatemala.

The resignation of Arbenz, Foster Dulles told Republican legislative leaders, was "a great triumph" for American diplomacy.[11] Could even so righteous a man have been oblivious to the irony of that remark?

Four

"No man on earth knows what this job is all about," Eisenhower once said of the presidency. "It's pound, pound, pound. Not only is your intellectual capacity taxed to the utmost, but your physical stamina."[1] Never was that truth more evident than in the eventful year of 1954, only Eisenhower's second in the presidency. The Supreme Court was readying its response to *Brown v. Board of Education of Topeka*, the important school desegregation case, with little but trouble in store no matter which way the decision went. A contentious Republican Party showed as much interest in revenge for the Democrats' twenty-year rule as in the Eisenhower legislative program. France was importuning the United States for aid in its losing war in Vietnam and dragging its feet on the rearmament of Germany. The "New Look" in defense had to be implemented over the not inconsiderable opposition of the Joint Chiefs. A series of H-bomb tests on Bikini atoll alarmed the world, including the U.S. public, about the potential of radioactive fallout. The Chinese were threatening Quemoy, Matsu, and Formosa, the Republic of South Vietnam was being more or less established, and the Southeast Asia Treaty Organization was under construction. In Guatemala, Eisenhower, the CIA, and Anastazio Somoza were ushering in decades of murder and repression.

As if there were not already enough on the president's plate, Defense Secretary Charles Wilson called him on December 2, 1953, to report that William Borden, formerly the staff director of the Joint Congressional Committee on Atomic Energy, had revived an old charge that J. Robert Oppenheimer's past associations made him a security risk.

Oppenheimer, formerly the head of the wartime Manhattan Project, the developer of the atomic bomb, was then Eisenhower's appointee to head a group advising the president what to do about the arms race. Among many of the world's scientists, Oppenheimer had won respect without parallel. Borden had no new evidence but brazenly charged anyway that Oppenheimer was "more likely than not [to be] a Communist spy."

The president was less disturbed by this wild, mostly unsubstantiated charge than by the possibility that the brash Red-hunter, Senator Joseph McCarthy of Wisconsin, might get hold of it. "We've got to handle this so that all our scientists are not made out to be Reds," Eisenhower told Hagerty. "That goddamn McCarthy is just likely to try such a thing."[2]

The day after Wilson's call, the president met with Lewis Strauss, whom he had appointed chairman of the AEC, and other officials. Eisenhower claimed that he was not "in any way prejudging" the Oppenheimer matter, but that he wanted a "blank wall" placed between top-secret information and the nation's number one wartime scientist, pending a formal investigation. Still ostensibly not prejudging, he said he saw "no evidence that implies disloyalty on the part of Dr. Oppenheimer," but that that did not mean the physicist "might not be a security risk."[3] So he proceeded to name a special three-member panel to look once again into whether J. Robert Oppenheimer of the Manhattan Project was a security risk — all, of course, in secrecy.

Eisenhower's willingness to lay this burden of internal suspicion on Oppenheimer is all the more striking in that the president actually agreed with the scientist that a nuclear arms race was madness, and that the only nuclear armament the nation needed was a force sufficient to deter the Soviet Union from attacking the United States or its allies. Most of the president's major advisers — Foster Dulles, for instance, Strauss, and the Joint Chiefs — wanted a clear American advantage in numbers of nuclear weapons, even if that meant nothing in terms of deterrence.

The obvious flaw in their approach was that Soviet men of like mind were unlikely to accept such an American advantage — hence an arms race was bound to ensue. As a consequence of his advisers' myopia, Eisenhower almost alone developed his "Atoms for Peace" proposal. On December 8, only five days after erecting that "blank wall" against Oppenheimer, the president asserted to the UN General Assembly that to allow the arms race to continue "would be to confirm the hopeless finality of a belief that two atomic colossi are doomed malevolently to eye each other indefinitely across a trembling world."

In forthcoming four-power talks, he continued, he would propose that the atomic powers (then the United States, the Soviet

Union, and the United Kingdom) contribute fissionable materials — five units from the United States to every one from the Soviets — to a new International Atomic Energy Agency under the UN. The new agency, drawing on scientific knowledge from all nations, would study means of putting atomic power to peaceful uses — especially providing electricity to areas in desperate need of it. In that way, Eisenhower said, "the miraculous inventiveness of man" need not be "dedicated to his death" but could be "consecrated to his life."

The General Assembly and most of the world cheered. But the Soviets stalled and eventually let Eisenhower's Atoms for Peace plan die, apparently fearing that acceptance would strengthen the U.S. lead in atomic weaponry. The president was profoundly disappointed, especially since his was the first American disarmament proposal not deliberately stacked against Moscow — sure to be rejected. When the Soviets still did not accept it, Eisenhower's attitude toward them and the Cold War hardened perceptibly.

Meanwhile, the Oppenheimer case was in the background of a continuing battle with Senator McCarthy. That was one reason why Eisenhower was reluctant to denounce the senator, who charged in March 1954 that development of the hydrogen bomb had been delayed by "Reds in the government." That was too close to Oppenheimer — who had indeed opposed construction of the H-bomb, on grounds that it added nothing to the nation's deterrent power.

After weeks of closed hearings, the Oppenheimer panel delivered in late May 1954 a two-to-one decision that, though the director of the Manhattan Project was not disloyal, his security clearance should be cancelled anyway, owing to "fundamental defects of character." By 4 to 1, the AEC upheld the verdict. The matter necessarily became public, much of the scientific community and many Americans were outraged, but at least — Eisenhower apparently thought — McCarthy had been kept out of the game.

Though he may not have wished to prejudge Oppenheimer, Eisenhower wound up seeming more nearly to believe than disbelieve Borden's charges. On June 1, as the president practiced his putting on the White House green installed for him, Hagerty came out to inform him that Oppenheimer intended to appeal the verdict.

"This fellow Oppenheimer is sure acting like a Communist," Eisenhower observed. "He is using all the rules that they use to try to get public sentiment in their corner on some case where they want to make an individual a martyr." He and Hagerty agreed that the most "damning" testimony had been that Oppenheimer had visited an old friend, Haakon Chevalier, after Chevalier may have tried to pick up security information for the use of a foreign government.

Eisenhower rather angrily wanted to know "how can any individual report a treasonable act on the part of another man and then go and stay at his home for several days?"[4]

He had little time to ponder that question or any other aspect of the Oppenheimer matter. Barely two weeks earlier, the Supreme Court had forced his attention to the kind of domestic upheaval no one in Abilene, Kansas, would have dreamed of in Dwight Eisenhower's formative years.

On May 17, 1954, the Supreme Court ruled unanimously that "separate but equal" public schools, then being operated in seventeen southern and border states and in certain school districts of Arizona, Kansas, New Mexico, and Wyoming, were not only actually but "inherently unequal," and thus unconstitutional. That ruling — in *Brown v. Board of Education of Topeka* — was a great achievement for the nation, for the Court, and for its new chief justice, Earl Warren of California; but it led to a significant failure by President Eisenhower, even as it set off a near-revolutionary civil rights struggle that was to alter the nation.

Eisenhower was not hostile to blacks or oblivious to their problems; nor was he a "weak" president, as Koreans and Iranians by then could testify. He knew that some presidents had found in the office implied and inherent powers beyond those specified in the Constitution, and he was aware of the possibilities of what Theodore Roosevelt had called the "bully pulpit."

He was, however, a strict constructionist of the presidency, wary of using its merely implied powers injudiciously — particularly to advance lofty but not universal causes. In his view, the executive branch was *required* by the Constitution to enforce the judiciary's decisions, but not to approve of or tout them. William B. Ewald, who served in the administration and later helped prepare Eisenhower's memoirs, wrote in his own book that the president "never saw himself as a moral dictator . . . he had a role to play, a role with prescribed powers he would not evade, prescribed restrictions he would not exceed."[5]

Probably more to the point, Eisenhower told speechwriter Arthur Larson years later, "I personally believe the decision [in Brown] was wrong," and that the Supreme Court should have required only "equal opportunity" rather than integration — the argument of the more enlightened southern opposition.[6] Herbert Brownell, who enthusiastically supported the Brown ruling, had perceived, even before Eisenhower had announced his intention to become a presidential candidate, that the author of Crusade in Europe was not likely to lead a civil rights crusade at home.[7]

Eisenhower did not, however, shirk his constitutional responsibility for *Brown* and he certainly was not unconcerned with its consequences. "The Supreme Court has spoken," he immediately told a news conference, "and I am sworn to uphold their — the constitutional processes . . . I will obey."

He already had played a crucial role, though at one remove, in the Court's decision. His cabinet headhunters, Clay and Brownell, might have persuaded Earl Warren to become secretary of the interior, probably taking Warren out of the picture, but Warren rejected the offer. Later, when the chief justice's chair unexpectedly came open before an associate justice's seat, Eisenhower might have nominated John Foster Dulles, but he considered Dulles too old to serve on the Court. He also thought about elevating Associate Justice Harold Burton, a Republican, and Associate Justice Robert Jackson, a Democrat, and considered Chief Justice Arthur Vanderbilt of the New Jersey Supreme Court, and Federal District Judge Orrie Phillips, a personal acquaintance.

Actually on his short list for the chief's chair was Federal Judge John J. Parker of South Carolina, who had been rejected by the Senate when nominated to the Court by President Herbert Hoover.[8] In 1955, Parker — still on the district bench — was to hand down for a three-judge court a crucial dictum declaring *Brown v. Board of Education* to mean that "[t]he Constitution . . . does not require integration. . . . It merely forbids the use of governmental power to enforce segregation." Most southern resistance to *Brown* was to be based on the distinction Parker cited.

What might have happened had Eisenhower nominated any of these men as chief justice, or had Warren gone to the cabinet, can never be known — except that it almost certainly would not have been what did in fact transpire after the president nominated Earl Warren to be chief justice.

In early 1953, Brownell, the new attorney general, was seeking the right man to serve as solicitor general — the Justice Department's litigator. Eisenhower suggested Warren, thinking the office would provide the governor of California with experience for the future service on the Supreme Court that the president fully intended him to have (see chapter 2). Warren accepted the job and began to wind up his affairs in California. But before he could be announced as the new solicitor general, Chief Justice Fred Vinson, Harry Truman's friend and appointee, died of a heart attack, in September 1953.[9]

Eisenhower and Brownell had concluded that the new chief justice should be a man with proven success in public life and with broad public acceptance of his integrity and competence, citing as a model former president, later chief justice, William Howard Taft (Senator Robert Taft's father). That conclusion favored Warren, a popular and effective governor, three times a presidential contender, once the Republican vice presidential nominee.

Brownell flew to California to consult Warren and quickly learned that the governor regarded Vinson's former seat as chief justice now open, as "the first vacancy" on the Court; clearly, he wanted to replace Vinson — pointing out that he already had made arrangements to leave Sacramento for the solicitor general's post, and could therefore join the Court immediately.

The following day, the president nominated Earl Warren to be chief justice of the Supreme Court — a selection many historians might designate as Eisenhower's most significant domestic act, certainly one that profoundly influenced the *Brown* ruling, one of the more revolutionary developments in modern American history.

Eisenhower called Warren "one of the finest public servants this country has produced." But not everyone approved the appointment — for instance, a former president of the American Bar Association who called on the president "to cease the unconscionable practice of putting politicians on the federal bench." Right-wing Senator "Wild Bill" Langer of North Dakota, chairman of the Judiciary Committee, held up confirmation, but Brownell believed Langer was unhappy less at the Warren choice than that his nominees for several post-masterships in North Dakota had been ignored by the White House. To his private diary, the president confided that if Republicans repudiated Warren "I shall leave the . . . party and try to organize an intelligent group of independents."[10]

There can be no doubt of his sincere conviction that Earl Warren would be a great chief justice. But how that greatness might be demonstrated, the president apparently had no solid idea — though he certainly knew that *Brown* was pending. The Vinson Court had heard argument in the case in December 1952, a month after Eisenhower was elected, but in June 1953 that Court deferred final judgment until a second hearing it ordered for October and later continued to December 1953.

Langer persisted in delaying Warren's confirmation but, acting on a precedent unearthed by Brownell and with the approval of Felix Frankfurter and other justices, Warren took his seat anyway — with Eisenhower in attendance — at the opening of the Court's term on October 5, 1953. He was not actually confirmed by the Senate until March 1, 1954; but had he waited until then to don his robes, he would not have been present for the second hearing of *Brown v. Board*, which began on December 7, 1953, or for his remarkable work in later obtaining the support of a unanimous Court against segregation in the public schools.

Generations of Americans have come to adulthood and citizenship in the near half-century since May 17, 1954; to many of them the questions facing the Supreme Court in its three-day rehearing of *Brown* in December 1953 and in its lengthy deliberations in early 1954 may seem to have been cut and dried. Of course, segregated schools were unconstitutional. Some members of the Warren Court may have felt that way, too — but not all of them. And, of course, the Supreme Court's interpretations of the Constitution are the law of the land — but in 1954 that was not universally and everywhere accepted.

Thurgood Marshall — lead attorney for the plaintiffs — had theorized that of the old Vinson Court he could count on only four votes against segregation: those of Truman's appointees, the midwesterners Sherman Minton and Harold Burton, and two of Roosevelt's choices, Hugo Black and William O. Douglas. Frankfurter thought Marshall would win at best a five-to-four decision — Frankfurter himself joining the four that Marshall thought he could count on. At the conclusion of the Warren Court's first judicial conference on the case, on December 12, 1953 — after the second hearing — there *was* a five-man vote to end segregation, but it did not include Felix Frankfurter. Chief Justice Earl Warren had joined Marshall's predicted four, but Frankfurter thought he needed greater historical justification. The only agreement the justices could reach that day was an important one — to keep discussing the matter among themselves and in the privacy of the conference room.

President Eisenhower was not alone in what we know now was his reluctance to see school segregation ended. Everywhere in the nation, de facto segregation — not supported by law but resulting from circumstances — existed and sometimes flourished, particularly in residential housing. If school segregation were to be banned, what about segregation in other walks of life? To most blacks in 1954, *Brown* was long overdue; but to the general run of white Americans, particularly in the South, the idea of "equality" of the races was nonexistent; and many would have shared the apprehension of Supreme Court Justice Stanley Reed: "Why — why, [desegregation] means that a nigra can walk into [a] restaurant . . . and sit down to eat at a table right next to Mrs. Reed."[11]

The case *for* segregation — which was not, in the early 1950s, generally considered disreputable — was impressively argued in both Supreme Court hearings by John W. Davis, a renowned lawyer who had been the losing Democratic presidential candidate in 1924. The second *Brown* hearing was the last of Davis's many appearances before the high court and he staged an able valedictory, scoffing at Thurgood Marshall's evidence that segregation damaged blacks psychologically — "fluff," Davis called such theories — pointing out that in Clarendon County, South Carolina, black pupils numbered 2,800 and whites only 300. Desegregation, therefore, would mean that in classrooms of 30 students in Clarendon, there would be roughly 27 blacks and 3 whites.

"Would the terrible psychological disaster being wrought, according to some of these witnesses," Davis asked, ". . . be removed if [the black child] had three white children sitting somewhere in the same schoolroom?"[12]

Earl Warren did not let such questions interfere with his firm opposition to supposedly "separate but equal" schools that were, in conception as well as fact, nowhere near equal. After the hearing and the inconclusive Court conference on December 12, Warren got down to work to bring around the four unpersuaded justices. He knew that a unanimous decision would carry greater weight with the public than a split on the Court — and that as much weight as possible would be needed if the public were to accept what would be perhaps the most controversial ruling in the Court's history.

Northern whites — few enthusiastic about desegregation anyway except as it applied to redneck customs depicted in *Tobacco Road* — provided only lukewarm support. After the December hearing, the *Brown* case quickly faded from the headlines. Some southern governors were known to stand so solidly behind segregation of the races that they might well challenge the Court's authority. The president was silent, and Congress, then dominated by a coalition of southern Democrats and conservative Republicans, on balance, was as much a hindrance as a help.

Warren, however, went steadily about his work in the quiet marble halls of the Supreme Court building, assigning himself to write the opinion — which, he later told his colleagues in a memo, he prepared "on the theory that [it] should be short, readable by the lay public, non-rhetorical, unemotional, and, above all, non-accusatory."[13] He considered all his colleagues — save, perhaps, Reed — persuadable, and so they proved to be when he lavished personal attention and his considerable political and persuasive skills upon them. Even Reed: Chief Justice Warren convinced him that a dissent would encourage southern resistance and therefore cast doubt on the Court's legitimacy.

The written draft of Warren's opinion finally assured Reed and others that school districts in the South would be given time to dismantle segregation — not forced to meet a quick deadline. On May 15, a conference of the justices gave unanimous approval to Warren's draft, with only minor revisions, and the chief justice was able to read his opinion to a packed court-room on May 17.

The stunned staff of the NAACP in New York, which — without much hope — had forced the *Brown* litigation, "just sat there looking at one another" in awe. Even cautious Thurgood Marshall thought the ruling meant that segregation could be eliminated everywhere within five years. Robert Jackson — not the justice but a history professor at all-black Virginia Union University — observed that his students "reacted as if a heavy burden had been lifted from their shoulders. They see a new world opening up for them."[14]

Unfortunately, the general public reaction to *Brown* meant that, for most, the new world would be a long time coming.

In the long months of achieving Court unanimity, Chief Justice Warren had received no help at all from the thirty-fourth president of the United States, the man who had appointed him to the Court. And on May 18, the day after Warren read the ruling, Eisenhower commented to Hagerty that he believed the decision was too sweeping. He'd tell reporters, he said, that of course a Supreme Court ruling had to be enforced and that he had sworn to do so. But, according to Hagerty's diary entry, the president was "concerned, as are all of us, on the effect of the ruling. There is a strong possibility that some of the southern states will take steps to virtually cancel out their public education system and turn to state-aided 'private institutions.' The President fears such a plan would handicap Negro children but [also] would work to harm 'poor whites.' "[15] (This was prescient; it also was the kind of reasoning segregationists offered.)

Eisenhower scrupulously avoided encouraging southern diehards to resist the law of the land. Later, in 1957, he acted strongly to enforce the Court's ruling when Governor Orval Faubus of Arkansas literally resisted by deploying the state's National Guard troops around Little Rock Central High School. Faubus and other segregationist leaders may have thought that Eisenhower's silence tacitly suggested that the president would look the other way when they issued their manifestos and passed their backward-looking laws. If so, they were grasping at a straw; on that point the president had spoken plainly enough: he would enforce the decision as he was sworn to do.

The real criticism invited by Eisenhower's silence on the *Brown* ruling, particularly with a half-century's hindsight, is that he *did* occupy a powerful moral position, he *was* a profoundly respected leader and individual, and by 1954 the argument against racial segregation was both clear and simple: *It was wrong.* Those questions of practicality that had so bothered the Supreme Court and many other Americans — including Eisenhower — could not change the overriding fact that in the twentieth century, nearly a hundred years after Appomattox, a decade after the great triumph of democracy in World War II, the land of the free and the home of the brave could no longer sustain, much less defend, legally enforced racial inequality. Was not the president of the United States therefore obligated to speak out against the darkest remaining stain on the history of the American people, the most threatening cloud above their future?

With his wartime victor's laurels, with his high moral standing, his popularity, and his immense prestige, Dwight Eisenhower might well have swung most of the nation into acceptance, however reluctant, of the Supreme Court's interpretation of the Constitution. That Eisenhower did not speak from the bully pulpit, or anywhere else, against school segregation and in defense of equality suggests, therefore, that the fundamental reason for his silence was not practical objection to a "too sweeping" decision but a reflection of his genuine view, the one he gave to Arthur Larson: that the decision was "wrong" in substance. Larson was scarcely an Eisenhower critic, and he only drew that conclusion after hearing the president say that he did not want a Negro to "court my daughter," and that he did not find "compelling" the theory that "separate" was "inherently unequal."

As president, Eisenhower "was neither emotionally or intellectually in favor of combating segregation in general," Larson decided. "It was not merely that he thought the Supreme Court school decision was wrong; he thought that the underlying theory on which it was based was also wrong."[16]

Eisenhower's admiring biographer Stephen Ambrose reluctantly concluded that the president's failure to lead in this instance was "almost criminal."[17] It was surely what should have been least expected of Dwight D. Eisenhower: a failure of duty — and not merely a passive failure, either.

Earl Warren's memoirs record that in the spring of 1954, before the *Brown* decision was announced on May 17, Eisenhower descended to *ex parte* tactics at one of the stag dinners he liked to give in the White House. Both Warren and John W. Davis were guests and seated near each other. After dinner, the president confided to the Chief Justice what was surely an improper suggestion about a case pending before the latter's court: "These [southerners] are not bad people. All they are concerned about is to see that their sweet little girls are not required to sit in school alongside some big overgrown Negroes."[18]

Writing long after, Warren may not have quoted Eisenhower's words verbatim, but he could hardly have mistaken their meaning. If Warren knew the remark was legally improper, he — a Californian — may well not have understood that in 1954 it precisely expressed southern paternalism, the southern stereotype of black men, and the southern paranoia about interracial sex. Eisenhower had used a classic expression of southern racism, one that anybody living in the South in the twentieth century must frequently have heard.

William B. Ewald has attempted to clean up this event, though even he records the telling memory that he heard Eisenhower say "the identical words *a decade later*" (italics added). Ewald thought they reflected no more than a "regional concern." That at the stag dinner the president was "nefariously lobbying against desegregation," he wrote, was "unthinkable"; and he quoted Brownell, another guest at that dinner, as saying that Earl Warren was "a stubborn Scandinavian," could hold a grudge, and "always thought someone was out to get him."[19]

Ewald believes that Warren deliberately slanted the stag dinner anecdote out of his "bitterness" and his "capacity for pettiness." Warren had good reason, of course, to be bitter at the failure of the president to support not just the unanimous decision Warren had labored so hard to achieve, but racial equality in the world's greatest democracy.

Eisenhower once said to Arthur Larson that a nation's "moral posture" was inevitably a part of its power.[20] If he seemed to ignore that truth in his opposition to *Brown*, that can only be seen as a moral failing and a lack of vision in a president who seldom suffered from either.

Five

In January 1954, the Department of the Army's general counsel, John Adams, sought the advice of Eisenhower's principal political advisers — Attorney General Herbert Brownell, United Nations Ambassador Henry Cabot Lodge, and White House Chief of Staff Sherman Adams (no relation to John). The four men, with Gerald Morgan of Eisenhower's congressional liaison staff, met in Brownell's office on January 21, 1954 — a meeting that brought about Eisenhower's sweeping proclamation of what was to become known as "executive privilege" and one that marked the beginning of the end for Joe McCarthy.

Neither McCarthy's subjugation nor executive privilege was John Adams's primary purpose. Instead he wanted advice about the army's response to the senator's plan to subpoena testimony from members of the army loyalty and security board. In discussing this matter, Adams outlined the details of influence-seeking by McCarthy and Roy Cohn on behalf of David Schine

— then a private in the army but formerly employed by the McCarthy subcommittee staff, a member of a wealthy Republican family, and Cohn's partner in 1953 in a spectacular tour of U.S. Information Agency libraries abroad. The tour had earned big headlines, and much derision, for its grab bag "discoveries" of allegedly subversive literature in these libraries. A State Department worker had been fired for labeling Cohn and Schine as what they were: "junketeering gumshoes."

Schine had been drafted in mid-1953. But, Adams related, beginning in July, McCarthy, Cohn, or other subcommittee aides sought numerous special privileges for their former colleague — even including demands for his relief from KP duty. Eisenhower's political advisers immediately recognized that these efforts provided explosive political ammunition against McCarthy himself. John Adams was therefore put to work drafting a chronology of all attempts to obtain special favors for David Schine.[1]

McCarthy and the Eisenhower administration in its first year had been something like uneasy allies — barely tolerating each other, if at all, only out of Republican

110

political necessity, each with high popular favor reflected in the polls. McCarthy, the scourge of subversives and the Democrats he charged had tolerated them, wanted Eisenhower and the new administration to be as ruthless as he in seeking and dismissing suspected Communists from the government. Eisenhower, though a hardline anti-Communist himself, had little sympathy with McCarthy's approach, considering it extreme and unfair.

On June 14, 1951, in one of his most intemperate speeches, McCarthy had blasted one of Eisenhower's great patrons, General George Marshall, for "losing China" through "a conspiracy so immense and an infamy so black as to dwarf any previous venture in the history of man." In the same speech, he assaulted Eisenhower, not then a Republican candidate, for not capturing Berlin in 1945 before the Russians did. That day, the SACEUR called McCarthy a "disciple of hate" — but only in his private diary. (Later, as president, Eisenhower termed McCarthy, in a graphic but mixed metaphor, "a pimple on the path of progress.")

In 1952, however, during his first news conference after coming home to seek the presidential nomination, Eisenhower had laid out a basic position that he was to maintain through thick and thin: "I'm not going in any manner or means to indulge in personalities" — publicly attack McCarthy or anyone else — and added that he was determined to prevent subversion "without besmirching of any man or condemning by loose association."

Later that year, in Milwaukee, the candidate omitted a defense of General Marshall (see chapter 1), to placate McCarthy's supporters.[2] And after he entered the White House in January 1953, he ducked or tactically declined several opportunities publicly to denounce the troublesome senator. McCarthy attacked Charles E. "Chip" Bohlen, for instance, after the president named Bohlen ambassador to the Soviet Union, charging that Bohlen was an "architect of disaster," owing to his role at the World War II Yalta Conference. This was widely considered an implied criticism of Eisenhower himself.

Without mentioning this attack, the president told the press that Bohlen was "the best qualified man . . . that I could find," adding that he knew Bohlen personally and well — thus refuting McCarthy's arrogant claim that Eisenhower might not realize what was in Bohlen's personnel file.

In that same early month of the new administration, McCarthy announced that he personally had negotiated an agreement with Greek shipowners not to transport goods to Communist China — keeping the talks secret to prevent "interference" from the State or Defense Departments. Harold Stassen, the new director of the Mutual Security Administration, declared that McCarthy in fact had "undermined" administration efforts to work out an even stronger treaty.

This appeared a good chance for Eisenhower to crack down on the freewheeling McCarthy. Instead, the president seemed to refute Stassen, on the remarkable ground that, since McCarthy had no power to negotiate a treaty, he could not have done so. The senator had only exercised any citizen's right.

On June 14, 1953, however, perhaps finally aroused by the "junketeering gumshoes" Cohn and Schine, and speaking without notes or text, the president implored his audience at Dartmouth College's commencement exercises: "Don't join the book-burners. Don't think you are going to conceal faults by concealing evidence that they ever existed. Don't be afraid to go in your library and read every book, as long as that document does not offend your ideas of decency. That should be the only censorship."

Adhering to policy, he did not mention McCarthy, Cohn, or Schine. But the speech drew an admiring response and was generally assumed to be a rebuke to McCarthy and his aides — until three days later, on June 17. In answer to a news conference query from Merriman Smith of United Press International, Eisenhower replied: "Now, Merriman . . . you have been around me long enough to know that I never talk personalities," and added, in less fatherly terms, "If the State Department is burning a book which is an open appeal to everybody in those foreign countries to be a Communist, then I would say that falls outside the limits I was speaking [of] and they can do as they please to get rid of them."

That didn't mean he approved of book-burning — "not exactly." But he certainly didn't want to "propagate Communist beliefs" with government money in government libraries.

These and other equivocal remarks caused widespread disappointment and led much of the press to charge that the president had backed away from the Dartmouth speech. Even the loyally Republican *New York Herald-Tribune* complained that the president apparently had withdrawn his objection to book-burning.

So it went in the first year of Eisenhower's presidency. He often was urged by some aides to confront McCarthy frontally, but Vice President Nixon and General Wilton Persons, the chief congressional liason, apparently were among a few administration "accommodationists" who wanted to get along with the senator. As an old Red-hunter himself, Nixon was able on one occasion to persuade McCarthy not to oppose James Bryant Conant, the president of Harvard, when Eisenhower named Conant to be High Commissioner in West Germany.

To his diary on April 1, 1954, Eisenhower confided that McCarthy was "so anxious for headlines that he is prepared to go to any extent." From this analysis, however, he again concluded that "nothing will be so effective in combating this particular kind of trouble-making as to ignore him. This he cannot stand." Still later, he wrote a personal friend that "nothing would probably please [McCarthy] more than to get the publicity that would be generated by public repudiation by the President."[3]

Right or wrong, and no matter how much leeway it granted to "this particular kind of trouble-making," Eisenhower resolutely continued his basic approach — appearing to ignore McCarthy. That policy, however, did not reflect the president's growing hostility to a man he personally despised.

No doubt with the aggressive senator in mind he had substituted a "security" program for the "loyalty" Harry Truman had claimed to uphold. "Security" could include a number of elements that did not necessarily mean disloyalty — homosexuality, for instance, or alcoholism might cause an otherwise loyal government employee to be labeled a security risk vulnerable to blackmail.

Security charges also were easier to prove than disloyalty; so by getting rid of generalized "security risks" rather than specific "subversives" the administration could cite higher numbers of persons discharged, and without the help of McCarthy's investigations. The administration enthusiastically played this numbers game but the security program also created morale problems among government servants, overloaded some agencies with the task of reviewing personnel files, and produced some McCarthy-like findings against basically innocent people.

Eisenhower seems, on one occasion, to have ventured cautiously into quasi-McCarthyite tactics himself. On November 6, 1953, Brownell told the Chicago Exchange Club that former President Truman had appointed Harry Dexter White to the International Monetary Fund *after* having been informed that White had been a member of a Soviet spy ring. White had then held the IMF job until he died of a heart attack, just three days after the House Un-American Activities Committee began to look into his case. Truman claimed that "as soon as we found that White was wrong we fired him," and the Democratic national chairman accused Brownell of "McCarthyism."

At a news conference on November 10 Eisenhower claimed to know little about Truman's supposed involvement. Brownell loyally shouldered the responsibility for the attack on Truman. But years later the former attorney general told Fred Greenstein, an Eisenhower biographer, that he had informed the president in advance about the Truman charge, and that Eisenhower had wanted his cabinet "to take the blows."[4] Brownell had agreed with that principle. Sherman Adams, in his memoir, claimed that the president had believed that the Brownell statement "would take away some of the glamour of the Mc-Carthy stage play."[5]

Perhaps specifically unknown to Eisenhower, but not without his generalized consent, McCarthy and other Congressional Red-hunters, like the House Un-American Activities Committee, had received considerable help in the early stages of the Eisenhower administration from the Justice Department, the Federal Bureau of Investigation, and its iconic director, J. Edgar Hoover.[6]

When Truman and the Democrats were in office, Hoover and the FBI had almost routinely fed information to zealous anti-Communist investigators in Congress. The FBI could not rely on the courts because much of its information was illegally obtained or from unsavory sources and would not sustain a legal indictment. Members of Congress, however, could expose "subversives" — the Bureau's aim — without regard to how or from whom the information had been obtained. Hoover insisted on strict secrecy about this Bureau relationship with Congress, threatening to cut it off if it were disclosed.

In 1952, when Eisenhower was elected president and carried Republicans into control of Congress, Joseph R. McCarthy entered his second term and became chairman of both the Senate Committee on Government Operations and its Permanent Investigations Subcommittee. Hoover, the craftiest of bureaucratic operators, assumed the new administration would support McCarthy so he could further expose the Democrats' alleged failures to root out subversives.

The FBI, therefore, with authorization from Deputy Attorney General William Rogers, continued for a time to work with McCarthy. But after the latter's attack on Chip Bohlen, Hoover's bureaucratic antennae vibrated, and he saw that his beloved FBI might be drawn into an Eisenhower versus McCarthy conflict, the new relationship began to unravel. By late summer 1953, fearing that the headlong McCarthy might recklessly expose the FBI's assistance and compromise it politically, Hoover broke off relations.

In September 1953, apparently at the height of his peculiar glory, Joe McCarthy — as if he had been appointed a sort of national security czar — informed willing listeners in the press that he had decided to pursue subversion in the military. So, even as he and Cohn began putting pressure on the army on behalf of David Schine, they opened a Red-hunting investigation of the Signal Corps laboratory at Fort Monmouth, New Jersey.

The senator's inquiries about subversion at Fort Monmouth intimidated the army and Secretary Robert Stevens, a mild textile manufacturer inexperienced in Washington and politics; thirty-three employees of the Signal Corps lab were suspended, on charges vague enough that most later had to be reinstated. But by January 1954, McCarthy was on to what he considered a far more newsworthy case, this one at Camp Kilmer, New Jersey — the promotion to major of a dentist named Irving Peress.

In civilian life, Peress had been a Communist (though a Trotskyite); drafted into the army, he at first lied about his past affiliation, then claimed Fifth Amendment protection. His promotion, as declassified army records have shown, was an administrative blunder; once all Peress's records were properly examined, he was given an honorable discharge — but not before

McCarthy's interrogation caused the dentist once again to "take the Fifth."[7]

Who promoted Peress? McCarthy demanded to know, and the question became a national byword, rather like an advertising slogan. But the matter turned ugly when in a one-man hearing in New York on February 18, McCarthy confronted Camp Kilmer's commanding officer, General Ralph Zwicker. A decorated hero of World War II, Zwicker in fact had recommended Peress's dismissal, not his promotion.

A sympathetic McCarthy biographer, Arthur Herman, has pointed out that the night before the hearing, McCarthy and his wife, Jean, had been in an automobile accident that sent her to the hospital and caused him to spend the night at her side. So he was not in a jovial mood and had had no lunch (but perhaps, Herman suggests, "several drinks") when the hearing opened.

When General Zwicker asked, in reply to one question, "Do you mean how do I feel about Communists?" McCarthy retorted, "I mean exactly what I asked you, General. . . . Anyone with the brains of a five-year-old child can understand the question."

McCarthy then asked if Zwicker thought

a general who had authorized an honorable discharge for someone he knew to be a Communist should be relieved of duty. Zwicker said no, and McCarthy erupted, "Then, General, you should be removed from any command. Any man who has been given the honor of being promoted to general and who says 'I will protect another general who protected Communists' is not fit to wear that uniform, General."[8]

Not with precise accuracy but not unreasonably, these charges usually have been interpreted as "bullying," in which McCarthy proclaimed that Zwicker did not have "the brains of a five-year-old child" and was "not fit to wear that uniform."

Secretary Stevens ordered Zwicker not to testify further, whereupon the unrepentant McCarthy ordered Stevens himself to the stand. Other Republicans warned that McCarthy would divert the issue from abuse of Zwicker to the army's blunder in promoting Peress.

"Joe will murder you," one senator told Stevens.[9]

McCarthy almost literally did. On February 23, Stevens — foolishly believing he was in a confidential meeting to work out a compromise — lunched with Senator

McCarthy and two members of his sub-committee, Karl Mundt and Everett Dirksen, in Dirksen's office. In what appears to have been good-faith naïveté, Stevens agreed to a compromise drafted by Mundt, by which the army secretary not only would let Zwicker testify again but would disclose the names of everyone involved in the promotion and honorable discharge of Irving Peress.

Tipped-off reporters, waiting outside to tell the world about the "compromise," knew Vice President Nixon's Senate office was next door to Dirksen's. So when they learned what Stevens had agreed to — in writing — they filed stories that led to such headlines as one in the next day's *New York Times*: "Stevens Bows to McCarthy at Administration Behest."

When the full import of what he had done dawned on the hapless Stevens, he tried to resign. Jim Hagerty, sympathetically aware that the administration had let Stevens walk into a "bear trap," talked him out of quitting. But Hagerty's boss was not so calm. "It's his army and he doesn't like McCarthy's tactics at all," Hagerty noted in his diary, and quoted the president as saying: "This guy McCarthy is going to get in trouble over this. . . . My friends tell me it won't be long before McCarthy starts using my name instead of Stevens'. He's ambitious. He wants to be President. He's the last guy in the world who'll ever get there if I have anything to say."[10]

A strong statement also was drafted — by Eisenhower himself, among others — for the chastened Stevens, in which the secretary denied that he had surrendered and promised to defend army personnel. Stevens read the statement to the press at the White House and Hagerty announced that the president "approves it one hundred percent." Later, in May, as a further demonstration of his support, Eisenhower took Stevens along on a trip to North Carolina.

Eisenhower's more important move in the wake of the Zwicker incident, however, came on March 2. He called Brownell, found the attorney general out of town, and spoke instead to Deputy Attorney General Rogers, requesting a legal brief on the president's power to order subordinates not to testify. He had taken the first, essential step toward his powerful doctrine of executive privilege.

Also on March 2, Secretary Dulles finally removed Scott McLeod, a McCarthy ally who had been the State

Department's controversial security chief. This was widely considered a rebuke to McCarthy — not least by McCarthy himself. At the president's news conference the next day, however, Eisenhower replied to a question about McLeod by saying, mildly enough, "Well, the assignment to duty of any administrative officer in any department is the responsibility of that department, and no one else's whatsoever" — no mention, as usual, of a senator named McCarthy.

This studied banality received, the next day, the following characterization in the *Washington Post*: "President Eisenhower said yesterday [the assignment of Scott McLeod] was not the responsibility of Joseph R. McCarthy." The president had opened that news conference with an innocuous call for "fair play" in Senate hearings, again without mentioning McCarthy. He had, however, included a tribute to General Zwicker, who had served under Eisenhower in the European theater. The headline in the *New York Times* proclaimed: "President Chides McCarthy on Fair Play in Hearings."

The press knew who Eisenhower was talking about and was not reluctant to say so, even if the president would not "engage

125

in personalities." Eisenhower understood that, and once told Lucius Clay that he counted on just such a press reaction: "I put it in talk, principle, and idea. They usually put it in headlines, 'The President spanks so and so.' "[11] Thus, the press, which bore so much responsibility for McCarthy's rise to prominence, also played an essential part in Eisenhower's more subtle efforts to bring him back to earth — not so much, in either case, deliberate role-playing as the press's response to clever political manipulation.

McCarthy was no pushover in that kind of feeding on the headline hunger of newspapers and broadcasters. In time to have his response included in next-day stories about Eisenhower's "fair play" remarks, the senator told a televised meeting of his subcommittee: "[I]f a stupid, arrogant, or witless man in a position of power appears before our committee and is found to be aiding the Communist Party, he will be exposed."

Neither side was backing down, as Eisenhower understood. To his cabinet on March 5 he sent a memo moving toward his evolving "executive privilege" stance:

Each superior, including me, must

remember the obligations he has to his own subordinates. These obligations comprise, among other things, the protection of those subordinates through all legal and proper means available, against attacks of a character under which they might otherwise be helpless.

At about this time, into what had been an essentially Republican conflict, waded the Democrats' recent presidential nominee, Adlai E. Stevenson. In a nationally televised address on March 6, Stevenson depicted the Republican Party as "hopelessly, dismally, fatally torn and rent . . . divided against itself, half McCarthy and half Eisenhower." The echoes of Lincoln's "house divided" speech and the strength of the charge — perhaps also its truth — angered Eisenhower; more important, the speech gave him the opportunity to argue that Stevenson had attacked *the party* and that therefore it was the party that should answer.

Swiftly he headed off McCarthy, who had demanded network time for a personal reply; Len Hall, the Republican national chairman, was instructed to seek time for a *party* reply instead, and Vice President Nixon was enlisted to make it. Frustrated,

McCarthy blustered that he would appeal to the Federal Communications Commission; Sherman Adams spiked that possibility (as White House chiefs of staff have ways of doing). Nixon then did his part by telling reporters that his speech would represent "particularly the view of the President, who is the leader of the Republican Party." In his televised speech on March 13, he made the essential point:

Men who have in the past done effective work exposing Communists . . . have by reckless talk and questionable methods, made themselves the issue rather than the cause they believe in so deeply . . . and have allowed those whose primary objective is to defeat the Eisenhower administration to divert attention from its great program to those individuals who follow these methods.

Coming from the nation's original and once most famous Red-hunter, that had authority. But Nixon could not restrain himself from a characteristic personal touch:

I have heard people say, "After all, we are dealing with a bunch of rats. What we ought to do is go out and shoot them." Well, I agree they are a bunch of rats. But just remember this: when you go out to shoot rats, you have to shoot straight because when you shoot wildly, it not only means that the rats may get away more easily — but you make it easier on the rats. Also, you might hit someone else who is trying to shoot rats, too.

With good reason, William Ewald thought this passage disclosed the speaker's "black id."

That same week, Edward R. Murrow's *See It Now* program on the Columbia Broadcasting System delivered a blistering attack on McCarthy's practices (a half-century later, Murrow's broadcast remains a landmark television event). The little-known Republican senator from Vermont, Ralph Flanders — apparently without instigation from the White House — rose in the Senate to proclaim that the junior senator from Wisconsin was "doing his best to shatter the party whose label he wears." At his next news conference, Eisenhower not only said that Flanders was "doing a service;" he allowed Hagerty to put his approving remarks "on the record."[12]

By far the most important event of the week, however, was the release by the army of John Adams's chronology of the McCarthy-Cohn efforts to win favorable treatment for David Schine. Hagerty believed the document could blow McCarthy out of the water. But the senator, ingenious as usual, turned the report on its head, calling it "blackmail" — the army's effort to curb his investigation into subversion.

The conflict had moved beyond simple resolution. On March 16, the McCarthy subcommittee voted to conduct a full investigation — in effect to choose between the army version and its chairman's response. A special counsel would be hired to replace Roy Cohn, who was a subject of the inquiry, and Karl Mundt would temporarily replace McCarthy as the presiding chairman. But could McCarthy retain a vote while being himself investigated?

Eisenhower's congressional liaison staff wanted to leave that question to the subcommittee, but the president, preparing for his weekly news conference, told the dissenters (in Hagerty's paraphrase): "I'm going to say he can't sit as a judge and that the leadership can't duck that responsibility. I've made up my mind you can't do business with Joe and to hell with any attempt to compromise."

To the reporters that day, the president actually said, "I am perfectly ready to put myself on record flatly . . . that in America, if a man is a party to a dispute, directly or indirectly, he does not sit in judgment on his own case."

The hearings then were all but ready to begin. McCarthy yielded on the question of his voting rights, naming his colleague, Henry Dworshak of Iowa, to cast his ballot, but he refused to give up his right to ask questions. Ironically, his interruptions were to hurt his cause far more than they helped. The subcommittee hired Ray Jenkins as counsel to the majority and the army brought in an experienced Boston lawyer, Joseph Welch, as its special counsel.[13] The Democrats' minority counsel was Robert Kennedy, a former McCarthy aide still somewhat devoted to the senator, but a bitter enemy of Roy Cohn.

The hearings began on April 22, 1954, when severe damage already had been done to McCarthy — by his intemperate blasts against General Zwicker, by the Murrow broadcast, by Ralph Flanders, and by Eisenhower's subtle but strong hostility, expressed mostly through the press and some Republicans in Congress.

The killer blow, however, was yet to come.

The McCarthy hearings of 1954 are remembered primarily for the dramatic display of indignation by the army's counsel, Joseph Welch, when the senator — gratuitously as it appeared, in bad faith as it was — charged on June 9 that one of Welch's young assistants, Fred Fisher, had been a member of the National Lawyers Guild, "the legal bulwark of the Communist Party."

"Until this moment," Welch memorably replied to McCarthy, "I think I never really gauged your cruelty or your recklessness. . . . Have you no sense of decency, sir, at long last? Have you left no sense of decency?"

This exchange was unquestionably the highlight of the hearings, one of the remarkable moments in television history, marking perhaps the lowest point Joe McCarthy ever had reached in public esteem. There's no reason to doubt the sincerity of Welch's outburst. It was not, however, exactly what it seemed and — shocking as the exchange was to viewers — it was not the major factor in McCarthy's downfall. That had come earlier.

When John Adams of the Department of the Army took the stand on Friday, May 14, and began to recount details of the pressures exerted on behalf of David Schine by McCarthy and his staff, Adams disclosed for the first time the meeting on January 21 in Attorney General Brownell's office. A puzzled Democratic member of the subcommittee, Stuart Symington of Missouri, asked why Henry Cabot Lodge, the ambassador to the United Nations, had been included in a meeting on a domestic political matter. Special Counsel Welch immediately broke in to say that the January 21 meeting had been a "high-level discussion of the Executive Department" and that Adams had been instructed not to testify as to the views exchanged at that meeting.

Instructed by whom? Even the Democrats were taken aback. "Does this mean we are going to get information about low-level discussions but not about high-level discussions?" Symington asked. The subcommittee adjourned, and Adams was instructed to come back on Monday, May 17, with his "instructions" in writing.

He brought a copy of a letter from President Eisenhower to Secretary of Defense

Charles E. Wilson that amounted to a legal brief setting out the sweeping new doctrine of "executive privilege." Executive departments were to furnish Congress, Eisenhower had written, full information about their policies but they were *not* to disclose "conversations, communications and documents" about how and why those policies had been reached "because it is essential to efficient and effective administration that employees of the Executive Branch be in a position to be completely candid with each other on official matters." In other words, if they feared their advice would be made public, they might not be "completely candid" and the president would not get their best advice. The letter to Wilson was the most sweeping and definite statement ever made of executive privilege as a doctrine of presidential leadership.

Here was the fruit of Eisenhower's call to William Rogers on March 2, requesting a brief on his power to prevent subordinates from testifying. In the immediate wake of the Zwicker incident, the president had started to prepare for the time when he could deny McCarthy the life's blood of his singular career — the power to delve into internal administration information. By May 17, the president was fully armed with the needed precedents and justification.

As John Adams showed the Wilson letter to the investigating subcommittee, the president, at the White House, already had laid down his new doctrine to Republican congressional leaders. He did not mince words: "Anyone who testifies as to the advice he gave me won't be working for me that night. . . . I will not allow people around me to be subpoenaed and you might as well know it now."[14]

When majority leader Knowland protested mildly that he did not like to see the subpoena powers of Congress weakened, Eisenhower repeated, "People who are my confidential advisers are not going to be subpoenaed."[15] Apparently chastened, Knowland later told the press that the leaders saw the new doctrine as a legitimate exercise of presidential power.

Not Joe McCarthy. He called the order an "iron curtain" and later announced that it was "the first time I've ever seen the executive branch of government take the Fifth Amendment."[16] And not the Democrats. Senator John McClellan of Arkansas called the executive privilege doctrine "one of the gravest mistakes this administration has made." McCarthy himself, outgunned for once, conceded: "I must admit I am somewhat at a loss as to know what to do at this moment."[17]

He was not long "at a loss," however; he seldom was. On May 27, he challenged outright the basic idea of executive privilege, announcing to the "two million federal workers" that "I feel it's their duty to give us any information which they have about graft, corruption, Communists, treason. . . . There is no loyalty to a superior officer which can tower above and beyond their loyalty to the country."

Once again, the senator had recklessly overstepped himself. Thus personally challenged, as Eisenhower probably never had been in his long career, and by a man who tacitly claimed equal authority and responsibility — perhaps even greater patriotism — the president lost his famous temper.[18] Hagerty records Eisenhower declaiming, as he strode about the Oval Office:

This amounts to nothing but a wholesale subversion of public service. . . . McCarthy is making exactly the same plea of loyalty to him that Hitler made to the German people. Both tried to set up personal loyalty within the Government while both were using the pretense of fighting Communism. Mc-Carthy is trying deliberately to subvert the people we have in government, the Constitution and their superior officers. I think this is the most disloyal act we have ever had by anyone in the Government of the United States.

When he calmed down, however, Eisenhower still did not want to "get in the gutter" publicly with McCarthy; he merely authorized Hagerty to issue a strong statement in Brownell's name:

The executive branch has sole and fundamental responsibility to enforce law and presidential orders. . . . That responsibility cannot be usurped by any individual who may seek to set himself above the laws of our land, or override orders of the President of the United States to federal employees of the executive branch of government.

Hagerty emphasized to the press that Eisenhower endorsed every word of Brownell's statement. That evening, May 27, Edward R. Murrow (no doubt encouraged by Hagerty) weighed in again, this time against "an elaborate system of informers" providing a senator with "stolen" information. And on June 17, speaking at Columbia University, Eisenhower himself denounced "those who seek to establish over us thought control — whether they be agents of a foreign state or demagogues thirsty for personal power and public notice."

The press, as usual, did the president's work for him, saying what he would not. The *New York Times* asserted that he had warned against demagogues "in an allusion to McCarthy."

The senator, meanwhile, had made few friends for himself by his demeanor during the televised hearings. His truculent manner, particularly his frequent "point of order" interruptions, became an unpleasant trademark. "The things that have hurt him," James Reston wrote in the *Times*, "are his manner and his manners . . . the Senator from Wisconsin is a bad-tempered man."

Biographer Arthur Herman has argued strongly, however, that McCarthy was "in terrible shape,

suffering from constant stomach complaints and sinus headaches. . . . Then there was the drinking. . . . What had been a shot of bourbon at work was now a tumbler. Where he had once relied on a surreptitious drink to get through a public speech, he now needed several to get through a morning of normal work. . . . When the hearings adjourned at 4:30 P.M. he would gather with his aides for several hours, then eat a hurried dinner before returning to the office to look at more files and plan strategy for the next day. . . . McCarthy would often sit up all night, shifting papers and sipping straight vodka until 6:00 A.M.[19]

No wonder the senator was ready to snap on the day of the Fred Fisher incident, June 9.[20] The matter had surfaced weeks before and a story about Fisher had appeared in the *New York Times*. In his diary, Hagerty notes internal discussion of the matter as early as April 2. Welch had judiciously removed Fisher from any committee duties, in order to avoid any possibility of compromising the army's case, and had made a deal with Roy Cohn: Welch would not bring up Cohn's alleged avoidance of the draft if Cohn would not mention Fred Fisher's membership in the National Lawyers Guild. McCarthy had agreed to this arrangement.

While the army counsel was questioning Cohn, however, he began in a teasing manner to urge Cohn to disclose "before sundown" the names of any Communists he might discover. Across the committee table, McCarthy, seeming to lose control, grabbed the nearest microphone. He did not, this time, have a "point of order" but began a rancorous statement:

"In view of Mr. Welch's request that the information be given, once we know of anyone who might be performing any work for the Communist Party, I think we should tell him that he has in his law firm a young man named Fisher."

"No, no!" Roy Cohn cried, but there was no stopping McCarthy.

". . . a young man named Fisher whom he recommended, incidentally, to do work on this committee, who has been for a number of years a member of an organization that was named, oh years and years ago, as the legal bulwark of the Communist Party . . ."

When he had finished, the room sat in silence while Welch, for a moment, composed himself — then launched into his famous reply. Still, when the old lawyer had finished his rebuke, McCarthy blundered on, talking about the Lawyers Guild, oblivious to the effect he had had on the committee and — more important — on the television audience. Mercifully, McClellan called for adjournment; thankfully, Mundt brought down the gavel. As the room emptied, McCarthy seemed to realize that he had somehow erred.

"What did I do?" he asked those around him.

The hearings had effectively ended, and were finally adjourned on June 17, 1954. The career of Joseph R. McCarthy, too, was near its end. A final rally in New York on July 28 gave him an ovation that lasted nearly three minutes but two days later Senator Flanders tabled a resolution of censure, the harshest rebuke the Senate can levy on one of its own. On August 3, by a vote of 75 to 12, McCarthy's colleagues voted to submit the resolution to a select committee — a jury of his peers. On September 27, the committee recommended censure.

After weeks of heated debate, with the White House maintaining a judicious silence, the entire Senate on December 2, 1954, approved, 67 to 22, the committee's recommendation — changing "censure" to "condemn." John F. Kennedy, Democrat of Massachusetts, who was in the hospital, was the only senator who did not vote.

After a pathetic appearance at the 1956 Republican National Convention, several bouts of detoxification, and three more years of ghostlike presence in the Senate that once had been his forum, Joseph R. McCarthy died on May 2, 1957 — a broken man renowned only for a word he had added to the English language: McCarthyism.

Historians probably never will settle the question whether Eisenhower's "strategy" against McCarthy was successful, more than any other would have been, or whether Eisenhower merely followed a long-established pattern in which he relied on others to do the dirty work of infighting and name-calling, in order to preserve his own high standing. In *RN*, his post-presidential memoir, Richard Nixon wrote that his speech answering Adlai Stevenson's "party divided" charge should have been made by Eisenhower. Nixon also quoted Walter Bedell Smith, Eisenhower's wartime chief of staff:

I was just Ike's prat boy. Ike always had to have a prat boy, someone who'd do the dirty work for him . . . do the firing or the reprimanding or give any orders which he knew people would find unpleasant to carry out. Ike always has to be the nice guy.

Jim Hagerty, Nixon, Brownell in the Harry Dexter White matter, Robert Stevens, various Republican senators, even Joseph Welch, can be seen as Ike's prat boys in the McCarthy battle. While letting others take on McCarthy publicly, the president always kept himself above the battle, secure in his vast popularity — but at the cost of the worst of the Red-hunting iniquities of the 1950s, suffered by many an American and by the good name of America itself.

Could some of these costs have been avoided by a firmer presidential stand by the national father figure? Even in hindsight, why should so prestigious a man as the victor of World War II have retreated so precipitously from the Marshall defense in Milwaukee in 1952 or the Dartmouth speech against book-burning?

Even if, however, the most damaging interpretation is put on Eisenhower's responses to McCarthy, the presidency as an institution, as well as his or any president's capacity to lead, may thereby have been preserved and possibly enhanced. In the forty years since Eisenhower left the White House, Americans all too often have had to learn, the hard way, that maintaining respect for the nation's highest office and its occupant is among any president's pressing duties.

That Eisenhower left the presidency a universally respected institution in 1961, that he was able to retire as a virtually unchallenged icon of public life — both speak strongly on behalf of his approach to McCarthy, however self-serving it also may have been, and even though it certainly did not meet the educational responsibility claimed for a president in his "bully pulpit."

Six

Eisenhower's second year in office — 1954 — came to an end on only one really sour note: in congressional elections that November, though the president had campaigned heavily, claiming an 83 percent success rate for his legislative program, Republicans lost seventeen seats in the House and two in the Senate. The Democrats took control of Congress and — though it could not be known at the time — were to retain it for the rest of Eisenhower's years in office. Only in his first two years, therefore, had his divided party — Old Guard vs. Modern Republicans — elected a congressional majority.

As the New Year, 1955, came around, however, the divisive McCarthy threat had been effectively ended, SEATO was up and running to balance the "loss" of North Vietnam, German rearmament had been achieved, Guatemala was "redeemed," the New Look was in place at the Pentagon, though still controversial with the public and among the armed services. A balanced budget was in sight, the legislative program seemed in good shape, and in various polls the president personally had an approval rating of 60 percent or better, not least because he had kept the peace (and achieved it in Korea).

Unknown to the public (and to most of the administration), however, Eisenhower had taken in secret one seemingly promising step that was to prove disastrous five years later. Because he had been unable to secure all the intelligence information he wanted from within the Soviet Union, he authorized, on November 24, 1954, the CIA and the Pentagon to split the $35 million cost of building thirty of the high-flying, long-range reconnaissance aircraft called the U-2.

In early 1955, however, the "ChiComs" (Chinese Communists) provided the major problem facing Eisenhower. In September 1954, they had begun shelling Quemoy and Matsu, small islands less than two miles off the Chinese coast, but strongly garrisoned since 1949 as outposts of Chiang Kai-shek's refugee Chinese Nationalist forces. In Chiang's major stronghold on Formosa (Taiwan), the old generalissimo dreamed unrealistically of returning to take control of the mainland, using Quemoy and Matsu as stepping-stones.

President Truman had ordered the Seventh Fleet to prevent a ChiCom attack on Formosa itself, and the order had been continued in force under Eisenhower. But it was not clear whether Quemoy and Matsu would be defended. After the shelling of the offshore islands began, the belligerent Radford wanted to land American forces on them and drop A-bombs on the mainland. Eisenhower had cooled him down, but in late October a mainland Chinese military buildup caused an invasion to appear imminent. The Joint Chiefs began their usual war dance; but the president told them he had no intention of going to war with China without congressional approval.

One day, Hagerty heard the president murmur, almost to himself: "Those damned little offshore islands. Sometimes I wish they'd sink."[1]

Instead, the crisis had intensified on November 13, when thirteen American fliers shot down over China during the Korean War were sentenced to long prison terms for alleged espionage. Outraged American protests followed and, partially to quell the uproar, Eisenhower signed a mutual defense treaty with Chiang — pointedly limiting it to Formosa and the nearby Pescadores, again leaving unclear his intentions regarding Quemoy and Matsu.

Even his steady hand was forced, however, when on January 10, 1955, the Communists bombed other islands, the Tachens, held by Chiang's Nationalists. With Dulles and the congressional leaders (now including Democrats like Speaker Sam Rayburn of the House), Eisenhower discussed a resolution empowering him to use armed forces to defend Formosa and the Pescadores, if necessary. Dulles wanted to include Quemoy and Matsu, too, but the resolution Eisenhower finally sought referred only to "such other territories as may be determined" — again leaving the world and the Chinese to guess what he intended about the offshore islands.

By large margins, Congress (by then Democratic but clearly respectful of a popular war hero president) provided the necessary resolution — the House acting within an hour of receiving Eisenhower's request. For the first time in history, Congress had authorized a war "in advance," at a time and place of the president's choice. (As with the secret U-2 decision, this triumph was to have an unhappy result in later years: President Lyndon Johnson used the Formosa resolution as a model for the Tonkin Gulf Resolution that in 1965 was to give him a virtual blank check to fight the U.S. war in Vietnam.)

At the time of the Formosa resolution's passage, Dulles set off new speculation about use of the atomic bomb when he spoke about "new and powerful weapons of precision" and later specified that the United States was prepared to use "tactical" atomic weapons in defense of Formosa — a statement cleared by the president. Eisenhower himself inflamed this debate with a news conference reply in which he said that "in any combat where these things can be used on strictly military targets and for strictly military purposes, I see no reason why they shouldn't be used just exactly as you would use a bullet or anything else."

Radford said that "war can break out at any time," and apparently was pleased with the prospect. Foster Dulles compared China's "aggressive fanaticism" to Hitler's, but Adlai Stevenson said Eisenhower was "risking a third world war in defense of these little islands." The controversy elicited from the president a famous remark: if asked about Formosa at an upcoming news conference, he told Hagerty, "Don't worry, Jim . . . I'll just confuse them."[2] He proceeded to do so, deliberately using the jumbled syntax for which he was already well-known to continue obfuscating his intentions in the Formosa Strait.

Even so, the Chinese apparently got the message — more openly stated in the "bullet" remark than when they had supposedly received the same notice in 1953, before agreeing to the armistice in Korea. At any rate, no invasion occurred, and on April 23, 1955, foreign minister Chou En-lai told the Bandung conference that China wanted no war with the United States, in fact was willing to negotiate. Eisenhower responded positively, the shelling of Quemoy and Matsu was ended, and United States and ChiCom representatives began inconclusive talks. The president never did have to say publicly, or perhaps even decide, whether he would defend the offshore islands, much less whether he really would use the A-bomb in doing so. Nearly a half-century later, with both Chiang Kai-shek and Chou En-lai long gone, Taiwan (Formosa) prospers, and still has not been invaded from the mainland.

Once again Dwight Eisenhower had done what the American people most wanted and expected from him: he had kept the peace — at least for the moment.

Still, there were two Germanys, two Koreas, two Vietnams, two Chinas, and even, in a sense, two Europes: for after West German rearmament and entry into NATO, the Soviets had responded with the Warsaw Pact, linking their satellite states in a defensive alliance and completing the postwar division of Europe into Eastern and Western blocs. No one could be sure, moreover, since Stalin's death, who was in charge in the Kremlin, or if anyone was. And as Eisenhower had predicted in his Atoms for Peace speech: "Two atomic colossi [seemed] doomed malevolently to eye each other indefinitely across a trembling world."

Americans, as a result, were having to accustom themselves to the frightening fact that their homeland security could no longer be taken for granted, as it had been for nearly two centuries. Intercontinental ballistic missiles and Polaris submarines were being built, as were their counterparts in the Soviet Union. Manned aircraft, with their obvious vulnerabilities, were no longer the only means of delivering atomic and nuclear bombs across what for so long had been guardian oceans and continents.

Pressures therefore were again building in Europe for a "summit" meeting to settle difficulties with the mysterious Soviet leadership. Foster Dulles and Eisenhower objected, until in May 1955 Moscow suddenly indicated willingness to sign an Austrian peace treaty. The president saw this as a signal of Soviet sincerity in seeking to avoid war, and a month later, a summit meeting to begin July 18, 1955, in Geneva, was announced by the two sides.

Along with the usual American goals, such as a unified Germany, that the Soviets were sure to reject, Eisenhower hoped for at least a beginning on a real disarmament plan. One of his White House assistants, Nelson Rockefeller, was asked for his ideas, and he put together a team of experts. Meeting at Quantico, they developed what became known as the "Open Skies" plan — the United States and the USSR would open their airspace to each other's full inspection, providing airbases and aerial photography facilities for the other's use, with the aim of preventing either side from building up a secret nuclear force or launching a surprise strike.

Anti-disarmament officials, including Secretary Dulles, objected vehemently — Soviet airbases on American soil? Impossible! When Rockefeller persisted in his unorthodox proposal, Eisenhower finally snapped at him: "Goddammit, Nelson, I've told you we're not going to do that. I don't want to hear any more about it."[3]

Before the president's party — including Mamie and John Eisenhower — left for Geneva, Eisenhower relented, adopted Open Skies for a formal proposal, and invited Rockefeller to come along. On July 21, 1955, with the conference making little progress on any front, Eisenhower unveiled Open Skies at the Palais des Nations — as he said, "to convince everyone of the great sincerity of the United States in approaching this problem of disarmament."

Nikolai Bulganin, chairman of the Soviet Council of Ministers, later told the conference that the idea seemed to have merit. But minutes afterward, First Secretary Nikita Khrushchev sidled up to say directly to Eisenhower, "I don't agree with the chairman" — thus telling the president not only that Open Skies was a nonstarter but that Khrushchev, not Bulganin, was at the moment the real power in the Kremlin.[4]

Khrushchev later said Open Skies was a "transparent espionage device" that Eisenhower "could hardly expect us to take . . . seriously"; and as Chip Bohlen observed in his memoir, the Soviets let the proposal "die of malnutrition."[5] Thus, what it might have accomplished, if anything, will never be known, but Open Skies was at least an imaginative break with the standard Western disarmament proposals *designed* by the Joint Chiefs to be rejected by the Soviets. The proposal also took account, whether or not deliberately, of Churchill's dictum not "to assume that nothing could be settled with Soviet Russia unless or until everything was settled."

The summit was not, however, a total failure, at least from the U.S. viewpoint. The president was able personally to observe that his old World War II colleague Marshal Zhukov was a broken man, a cipher in the Soviet leadership, that Bulganin was a front man, and Khrushchev the true boss. Eisenhower himself was established even more firmly as a world leader for peace. The summit also fostered briefly what speechwriters and journalists of the time liked to call "the Spirit of Geneva" — a friendlier, less warlike, more hopeful sentiment felt round the world in the midst of the depressing Cold War. In a state of mild euphoria, therefore, President Eisenhower and Mamie flew in August to her hometown, Denver, Colorado, for their 1955 summer vacation.

The golf and fishing were great and Eisenhower, for a change, had time to think about whether to run for a second term, despite advancing age, some health worries, and the allure of his farm at Gettysburg. Many of his friends came visiting, and there was plenty of opportunity for laughter, bridge, campfire cooking, and derision of the likely Democratic nominee, Adlai Stevenson.

Early on the morning of September 20, 1955, however, after a day of golf, office work at Lowry Air Force Base, and dinner at Mamie's mother's house, the president woke about 1:30 A.M. with a severe chest pain. The White House physician, Dr. Howard Snyder, was at his bedside within the hour, administering medicines and drugs that enabled Eisenhower to sleep until noon. Afterward, an electrocardiogram disclosed that he had suffered a coronary thrombosis, and Snyder ordered the president transferred to Fitzsimmons Army Hospital. There, to the world's alarm, he was installed in an oxygen tent.

In Washington, Jim Hagerty got the news via a call from his assistant, Murray Snyder (no kin to the doctor), at about 4:30 P.M. He notified Vice President Nixon, commandeered an air force plane, and few immediately to Denver. From Fort Belvoir, John Eisenhower also flew out, conferring first with his mother, who had moved into the hospital to be with her husband. In a corridor conversation, Hagerty told John that Dr. Snyder considered the heart attack "not severe but not slight either."[6]

The next day, the noted heart specialist Dr. Paul Dudley White, who had been summoned by Dr. Snyder, examined Eisenhower and confirmed Snyder's prognosis: the president, he said, had had "a slightly more than moderate heart attack — grade 3 out of five grades."[7]

Taking charge of press relations, Hagerty initiated with family and medical approval a historic policy of full disclosure of the president's condition, as described by Drs. Snyder and White. This policy was in sharp contrast to the secrecy that previously had blanketed presidential illnesses, like Woodrow Wilson's stroke in 1919 and Grover Cleveland's cancer operation in

1889. Full disclosure of Eisenhower's condition also was a departure from the unadmitted physical disabilities that had made Franklin Roosevelt's pursuit of a fourth term in 1944 medically unwise. Hagerty's informative regular bulletins for the White House press corps — which had transferred itself to Denver — also contrasted with the silence that officially but not entirely successfully covered an arcane political power struggle in Washington.

Vice President Nixon was historically next in line to succeed Eisenhower. Administration officials, particularly Foster Dulles, nevertheless feared that if Nixon appeared to be taking power even on an emergency basis, his never-dormant ties to the Old Guard would result in its capture of party leadership, or even of the administration. Dulles scotched any delegation of presidential powers to anyone and insisted that White House Chief of Staff Sherman Adams go to Denver, stay at the president's bedside, and see to it that Eisenhower remained in charge.

Conservative Republicans, notably Senator Styles Bridges of New Hampshire, urged Nixon to assume a sort of "acting president" role. Save for arguing unsuccessfully with Dulles that he, Nixon, should go to Denver instead of Adams, the vice president made no such effort. He wisely realized that if he were to become the actual president following Eisenhower's death, or the Republican candidate if Eisenhower could not run in 1956 — either of which at first seemed possible — he could be damaged politically by accusations of having attempted a power grab. So he managed rather adeptly to appear to be "filling in" for poor, sick Ike, rather than "taking over" the presidency. Presiding over cabinet meetings, for instance, Nixon carefully sat in the vice president's accustomed chair — not in the president's.

Fortunately, both the national and international scenes remained quiet as Eisenhower recovered rapidly. The president and his wife were able to return to Washington on November 11, less than two months after his heart attack, and went almost immediately to the Gettysburg farm for his further recuperation. But he had not regained health rapidly enough to quell speculation about whether he would run for a second term, and it was not until late February 1956, after numerous tests and assurances from his doctors, that Eisenhower finally said he would be a candidate for a second term.

One reason he so decided, Eisenhower conceded to himself, was that he had not groomed an acceptable successor. Foster Dulles, moreover, argued that Eisenhower was the world's most trusted man, its greatest force for peace; and so many others assured the president that he was indispensable that Eisenhower — never one to belittle his own worth — finally confided to his diary: "I suspect that Foster's estimate . . . is substantially correct."

That settled the presidency question, but not before some bizarre speculations by Eisenhower, the supposed "nonpolitician," about who the Republicans might nominate if he chose not to run. In conversation with Hagerty at Gettysburg, he mused aloud about Herbert Hoover, Jr., Charlie Halleck, William Rogers, Assistant Treasury Secretary Robert Anderson (a Texas Democrat but "just about the ablest man I know"), George Humphrey, Sherman Adams, Herbert Brownell, his brother Milton, even "the little man on the wedding cake," two-time loser Tom Dewey.[8]

Eisenhower's decision to run again fortunately mooted these pipe dreams — but raised another question: Nixon again? Since the so-called fund crisis in 1952,

Eisenhower had not been personally comfortable with Nixon. The two were not socially close, and though he admired the vice president's loyalty, intellect, and work ethic, the president considered Nixon too "politically minded" and doubted that he was "mature enough" — a constant, rather condescending Eisenhower concern about many of his associates, even including Dewey.

A number of polls suggested, moreover, that Nixon might cost Eisenhower votes in a campaign against Stevenson. And anyway, with a heart attack victim at the head of the ticket, the identity of his running mate would be of more than usual concern to the voters. So Eisenhower suggested that the vice president decide for himself whether to remain on the ticket or to take a cabinet post "to gain experience" for his expected presidential race in 1960.

Everyone, including Nixon — who was indeed politically minded — saw that this would appear to be a "dump Nixon" move, a demotion that might well end any chance Nixon had to be president, ever. Did Eisenhower know it, too? If he did, and it's hard to imagine that he did not, his suggestion could have been what Fred Greenstein called a "hidden-hand" way to rid himself of a man he did not want in the White House, without appearing himself to be harsh and ungrateful, or offending Nixon's political supporters.[9]

If Eisenhower did *not* understand that he was, in fact, proposing to dump Nixon — he insisted that he only wanted the vice president to get more "experience" in the cabinet — he was far less astute politically than usual, and less sensitive to the appearance of things. The Nixon-for-cabinet ploy made the president look politically inept and — perhaps worse — ungrateful to a loyal and deserving subordinate. Charles Jones, the oil tycoon and one of Eisenhower's bridge-playing friends, once demanded of the president while Nixon was twisting slowly in the wind: "Ike, what in hell does a man have to do to get your support?"

Eventually, Nixon swallowed his pride and told Eisenhower he would be "honored" to stay on the ticket; Eisenhower then swallowed his objections, and the 1952 ticket was set to do battle again — with what ordinarily would have been the twin handicaps of a physically impaired presidential candidate and an unwanted running mate. But it was Eisenhower who counted; the "man of peace" was all but a sure thing.

On Election Day, heart attack or no heart attack, Nixon or no Nixon, Americans gave the Republican candidates a ten million vote margin, double that of 1952 over Stevenson and his running mate, this time Senator Estes Kefauver ("the sorriest and weakest pair that ever aspired to the highest office in the land," in the president's ungenerous estimate).

For one of the few times in the history of presidential elections, even this landslide was overshadowed by news from abroad — war in the Middle East, uprising in Eastern Europe, and a rare break with three of the nation's most important allies, Britain, France, and Israel.

Part of a tangled story began in July 1956 when the Egyptian ruler, Gamal Abdel Nasser, recognized Red China and ordered arms from Communist Czechoslovakia. Incensed by this Cold War effrontery, Eisenhower and Dulles withdrew promised U.S. support for Nasser's huge Aswan Dam project. But Nasser could play tough, too; he nationalized the Suez Canal, promising to devote its revenue to building his dam. This offended the Victorian psyche of Britain's Prime Minister

Anthony Eden — finally playing the lead role after years as understudy to Winston Churchill. Eden professed not to believe the Egyptians could operate a canal vital to all maritime nations, and cabled Eisenhower that the West must be ready to use force, if necessary, to retake Suez.

The president, on the other hand, thought Nasser was "within his rights" to seize a canal running though his national territory, and scoffed at the condescending British notion that the Egyptians would not know how to operate it. The president urged Eden to calm down and go slow. Thus admonished, both the British and the French seemed to pressure Nasser only diplomatically until well into the autumn of 1956.

The U-2 reconnaissance plane had become operative, however, and one of its overflights of the Middle East finally gave Eisenhower an inkling of the truth — evidence that the French were arming the Israelis with Mystere jets, contrary to French commitments in a Tripartite Declaration with Britain and the United States that persuaded the president that a plot was afoot — Israel would attack Jordan, giving cover to a British-French armed takeover of Suez. He was right about the plot but wrong about Israel; the secret plan was for Israel to attack Egypt, not Jordan, while the British and French moved on the canal, pretending only to protect it. None of this included consulting or even informing the United States, which was in the quadrennial contortion of a presidential election.

With the Middle East about to erupt, as the U-2 gave Eisenhower reason to suspect, Eastern Europe stirred ominously as well. In Poland, an upheaval overthrew the Soviet-installed government in favor of one headed by Wladyslaw Gomulka, who promptly claimed there was "more than one road to socialism" and that the chosen Polish road would lead also to "democratization." In Hungary, demonstrations inspired by Polish defiance demanded the return to national leadership of Imre Nagy, whom the Soviets had thrown out in 1955.

Despite four years of Republican boasting about "liberation" to come, despite the fact that the administration had anticipated a Soviet satellite revolt someday, and had even encouraged it through radio propaganda heard in Eastern Europe, Eisenhower had known all along that the United States could do little to support an actual revolt in the satellites. When Hungary did reinstate Nagy, the Soviets sent troops and tanks into Budapest, and the Hungarians, resisting in the streets, learned for themselves, through blood, death, and defeat, that all Eisenhower would do was to issue a statement deploring Soviet intervention — while forbidding the CIA to air-drop arms and supplies to the Hungarians, lest the United States appear in Moscow to be aiding a satellite revolt and trying to break up the Warsaw Pact.

In late October, at an NSC meeting, Foster Dulles reported that Egypt, Jordan, and Syria had entered into a military pact and that he expected (owing, we now know, to faulty intelligence) an immediate Israeli attack on Jordan. Two days later, on October 28, 1956, while Eisenhower was making a campaign appearance in Richmond, Virginia, the stunning news broke: the Israelis had launched the expected attack and were driving ahead — not into Jordan, but across Sinai against Egypt.

Back in the White House that night, Eisenhower and his lieutenants belatedly grasped what was going on: when the Egyptians, under Israeli attack, closed the canal, as they almost certainly would, the British and French would move in as "protectors" and take it over, having concerted the plan with Israel. As would become clear, the British and French expected that their close relations and their NATO ties with the United States would force Eisenhower to support them. The Israelis counted on the importance of the Jewish vote in the concurrent American election to produce the same reaction.

Indeed, the president was badly surprised, partially owing to election distractions and intelligence failures, more importantly to the fact that he had not believed his old friends and allies would "double-cross" him (as someone might have said in the Western novels he liked to read). Eden, Israel's David Ben-Gurion, and the French premier, Guy Mollet, obviously had done just that. But it was then their turn to be surprised — because Eisenhower, in one of his finest hours as president, decided without hesitation to throw the weight of the United States *against* the plotters, even if they were friends and allies. He resolved to take a cease-fire resolution to the United Nations the next day, and he announced immediately that he would honor the Tripartite Declaration's pledge to support *any* victim of aggression in the Middle East.

The next day, October 29, in the UN

Security Council, Britain and France vetoed a U.S. resolution calling on Israel and Egypt to cease fire, for Israel to withdraw to its original borders, for all UN members to refrain from using force, and to join in an embargo on Israel until it did withdraw. The two European powers also issued an ultimatum that laid bare their plot: Egypt and Israel were to pull back ten miles from the canal to permit its occupation by Anglo-French forces, which then would keep the opposing armies apart. Israel, as planned, promptly agreed, aiming to keep Sinai and hoping Nasser would fall.

Appalled, Eisenhower cabled Eden and Mollet, urging them to cancel the ultimatum. In the House of Commons, Eden survived a vote of confidence by the narrow margin of 270 to 218. Meanwhile, the Soviets offered to withdraw from Budapest and cease interference in satellite affairs. Eisenhower, already mistrusting his allies, doubted Soviet sincerity, too. The next morning, October 30, Lodge phoned Eisenhower to tell him of a triumphant reception for the U.S. resolution that the British-French veto had nullified. In what would later be called the Third World, acclaim for this attempted U.S. policy —

supporting Egypt against Israel and against two of America's closest allies — was "absolutely spectacular," Lodge reported.

The policy may indeed have been splendid; it was not, when soberly considered, so surprising. Not only had Eisenhower chosen to support traditional (though not always observed) U.S. positions — the primacy of the UN, upholding the Tripartite Declaration, standing for the rights of nations — but he had been blatantly betrayed by the allies he now rebuffed. As for the British-French-Israeli plot itself, he flatly told Senator Knowland: "I think it is the biggest error of our time, outside of losing China."[10]

Eden nevertheless ordered the British strike to proceed — despite his near loss in the Commons and disregarding both world opinion and Eisenhower's opposition. On October 31, British aircraft bombed Cairo and Port Said and Nasser responded by sinking a cement-laden ship in the canal to block it — the first of an eventual thirty-three such hulks. Together with Syria's action in blowing up an important pipeline, the blockage of the canal effectively shut off the vital flow of Middle East oil to Europe.

In the United States, Election Day was

steadily approaching, but events overseas proceeded apace. On November 1, Allen Dulles of the CIA reported to the NSC that Nagy had withdrawn Hungary from the Warsaw Pact; and Dulles Foster lamented that just when the United States might somehow have exploited Communist difficulties in Eastern Europe, Britain and France, aided by Israel, had renewed Western colonialist policies in the Middle East and forced a break with the United States. Eisenhower ordered the secretary of state to introduce the American resolution to the UN General Assembly that afternoon. Then, in Philadelphia, making what was to be his last campaign speech, he again pledged to uphold the rule of law for both weak and strong nations.

His major weapon was not military but economic — an embargo on shipments of oil to Europe. Since no oil was coming in from the Middle East, Britain and France might soon strangle in an oil shortage and be forced to call off their attack on Egypt. In the next few days, however, the Western and Israeli drives continued, the Israelis conquering most of Sinai and Gaza and destroying the Egyptian air force. The General Assembly adopted the U.S. resolution, 64 to 5, Britain, France, Israel, Australia, and New Zealand opposing; but in the Security Council the Soviets vetoed another American resolution calling on them to withdraw from Hungary.

Then, disregarding their own "noninterference" pledge, the Soviets launched 200,000 troops and 4,000 tanks against Budapest. Nagy fled to the Yugoslav embassy but Hungarian "freedom fighters" still resisted — without even token U.S. military support. Foster Dulles, at this tense moment, had been forced to enter the hospital for an emergency cancer operation, Undersecretary Herbert Hoover, Jr., acting in his place.

On November 5, the day before the 1956 election, as if Hungary were not a sufficient problem for the Soviets, they took a meddlesome and threatening hand in the Middle East crisis. Western paratroopers had landed in Suez, and Nikolai Bulganin (still exercising at least limited authority in Moscow) told the three attacking nations that the Soviet Union might use force to restore peace, and seemed to threaten missile attacks on London and Paris. He also sent Eisenhower an astonishing letter proposing that United States and Soviet forces should enter Egypt and jointly put a stop to the Western-Israeli attacks.

Eisenhower and his aides considered the latter suggestion obviously "unthinkable" — but a sign also that the Soviets were both angry and scared, thus perhaps on the verge of "start[ing] something." If they did, a tired but calm president said, "We may have to hit 'em . . . with everything in the bucket."[11] But for the moment, he settled on having Hoover put out a statement that if the Soviets tried to send troops into the Middle East, the United States would resist in force.

On November 6, Election Day, with tension at its apex, the Eisenhowers drove to Gettysburg to vote. On their return, by helicopter, they learned that there had been no overt Soviet moves into the Middle East — hence there would be no immediate World War III. Eden, moreover, now claimed control of the Suez Canal and finally had agreed to accept a cease-fire; he also wanted a strong UN peacekeeping force to take over in Egypt. In the double-edged crisis in Eastern Europe and the Middle East, the worst was over.

Eisenhower called Eden to congratulate him on the cease-fire statement, and that night both leaders survived voting tests — Eisenhower with his landslide reelection, Eden in another close confidence vote in the House of Commons. By the end of November, the British and French were mostly out of Egypt, a UN force was in place, and in December the Egyptians started clearing the canal. The European oil crisis, effectively used by the president to bring pressure on his allies, was relieved when he raised the embargo on oil shipments. Both the NATO and the Warsaw Pact alliances had been preserved, hence World War III avoided, and U.S.-Soviet relations had been restored to a sort of normal hostility.

The price, of course, had been high. Ben-Gurion refused to withdraw from Sinai and Gaza; the Soviets captured and executed Imre Nagy, and the United States abandoned forty thousand dead freedom fighters, as well as innumerable Hungarian refugees, fleeing to the West at the rate of three to four thousand a day.

In the midst of the double crisis, Americans had confidently awarded Dwight Eisenhower a second term. But with the two "atomic colossi" still eyeing each other across an even more fragile world, he knew perhaps better than anyone that keeping the peace for another four years, let alone for the unpredictable future, would not be simple and perhaps not even possible.

Seven

Before the 1956 crises in Hungary and Egypt, Eisenhower and the Republicans had planned, with good reason, to run a classic peace-and-prosperity presidential campaign. After the mild recession of 1953–1954, unemployment had fallen sharply; in the fourth quarter of 1956, gross national product topped $420 billion; and that year even George Meany of the AFL-CIO conceded that "American labor never had it so good." Republicans could properly claim that "everything is booming but the guns."

They could also point to Eisenhower's significant first-term domestic achievements — for instance, the interstate highway system, of which the president was particularly proud; the Saint Lawrence Seaway, opening Chicago and the Great Lakes to ocean traffic; two years of balanced budgets; and a Refugee Relief Act that eased the reactionary McCarran-Walter Act of 1952. Other good things not directly products of the Eisenhower administration nevertheless had happened

173

on the president's watch: the Salk vaccine against poliomyelitis, an increased use of computers, nuclear power development, and the introduction of commercial jet aircraft.

There had been no such achievement, however, in the crucial field of civil rights, save for the Supreme Court's epic decision in *Brown v. Board of Education* — a ruling for which Eisenhower could take no credit and in fact had refused to endorse (and which the 1956 Republican platform merely "accepted"). Attorney General Brownell did work up a civil rights bill narrowly balanced between southern congressional opposition and contrary pressures from those Eisenhower called "radicals" on his White House staff. But the House, after prolonged debate, killed the bill's voting rights provision and its language establishing federal responsibility for rights enforcement; Missisippi's Senator James Eastland, chairman of the Senate Judiciary Committee, then throttled the measure's mild remaining elements — a civil rights division in the Justice Department, a bipartisan commission to look into racial disturbances. The net result: zero.

A minor administration "bricks and mortar" education bill also failed, largely because most of the money it would have provided to help the states with classroom construction would have gone to the South, where the segregated school system had not yet been dismantled. The most interesting issue of 1956 arose when Stevenson made the strategic error of challenging Eisenhower on defense, calling for a nuclear test ban. That was a matter with long-term and worldwide political resonance, but the president and former general dismissed Stevenson's proposal as "theatrical" — although the victor of World War II actually favored a test ban himself, and the possibility would become of major importance to him in his second term.

The twin foreign policy crises in Hungary and Egypt at the climax of the 1956 campaign overwhelmed all other political matters and, of course, favored an incumbent experienced in such matters; in the last weeks of the campaign, Stevenson and Kefauver might as well have stopped running. But once the street fighting in Budapest had petered out (though all those refugees still waited and hoped), and once oil and cargo flowed again through the Suez Canal, the domestic issue Eisenhower most wanted to avoid — civil rights —

flared anew, like a fire that refused to die out.

Eisenhower himself was partially responsible for fanning the blaze, by resubmitting Brownell's 1956 civil rights bill in its original, unemasculated form, to a Congress still dominated by southerners and their Old Guard Republican allies. The president professed to see the measure as purely an effort to guarantee the right to vote for all Americans, but Richard Russell of Georgia — in the Senate a deeply respected man — described it as "a cunning device" to force "the integration of white and Negro children."[1] At his news conference the next day, July 3, Eisenhower made a rare blunder, conceding that Brownell's bill contained "certain phrases I didn't completely understand." Thus invited to educate him, southern senators offered an amendment assuring jury trial for anyone charged with contempt of court in a civil rights case.

Juries are made up from voting lists, which in the South at that time were virtually all white. The amendment meant that few if any southern white men ever would be convicted by other southern whites for violating a Negro's rights. Eisenhower well understood that and appealed to Republi-

176

cans to reject the amendment. But on July 17, at another of his weekly news conferences, the president put his foot in his mouth again, declaring that he could not imagine "any set of circumstances" that would cause him to have to send federal troops to enforce a court order. Not only were some southerners therefore persuaded that the president would never act against them, he also had painted himself into a narrow corner, in the entirely possible event that such circumstances did arise — as they soon would, in remote Little Rock, Arkansas.

On August 2, 1957, Senate Majority Leader Lyndon Johnson of Texas managed to get the jury trial amendment passed, evoking Eisenhower's anger; millions of Americans, he said in a public statement, would continue to be disenfranchised as a result. For the next several days, the congressional press — a young reporter named Wicker among them — trooped back and forth between Senate and House, where the bill had passed *without* the jury trial amendment. They were trying to keep up with efforts to put together a compromise; ultimately and largely because of cordial relations between Democratic Speaker Sam Rayburn of Texas and House Republican Leader Joe Martin of Massachusetts, the final version did modify the jury trial amendment — but only slightly, allowing a judge to decide whether a defendant would or would not receive a jury trial.

Like Eisenhower himself, the final bill — important primarily as the first civil rights measure passed by Congress in modern times — took only a weak and contradictory stand on the most divisive issues of the era. It provided a Civil Rights Commission (but only for two years), a Civil Rights Division in the Justice Department, and empowered the attorney general to seek an injunction when someone was deprived of the right to vote. But its penalties were slaps on the wrist, and the compromise jury trial amendment would put few rights offenders behind bars. Eisenhower signed this flaccid measure but it never had much effect — and was soon overtaken by events in Little Rock.[2]

That city's school board, belatedly following *Brown v. Board*, had taken steps to integrate its Central High School. Arkansas Governor Orval Faubus, who was hoping for reelection, decided — perhaps influenced by the president's inconclusive remarks — to reap some easy political credit by blocking the entry of black students on the first day of school in September 1957.

He acted at first through a state chancery court, presenting evidence of increased gun sales in Little Rock. Federal Judge R. N. Davies denied the state court's jurisdiction and ordered integration to proceed. Faubus then called on the Arkansas National Guard to surround Central High, ostensibly to protect the black children scheduled to enter. Judge Davies repeated his order, but Faubus actually used the Guardsmen to turn away the blacks. Davies then ordered the Justice Department to investigate and Attorney General Brownell, postponing his desire to return to private practice, sent FBI agents into Little Rock. They soon reported that gun sales had *not* increased and that Faubus had *ordered* the Guard to prevent the black students from entering Central High.

Here were developing precisely those circumstances Eisenhower had told the press he could not imagine. Even so, he still hoped Faubus would see the light of reason and federal authority, and would retreat. Judge Davies was under no such illusion and ordered the Justice Department to file an injunction against the governor, who was instructed to appear before the court on September 20.

Representative Brooks Hays of Arkansas and Sherman Adams, the White House chief of staff — old friends from joint service in Congress — then consulted a group of southern governors, seeking a solution. Adams asked Eisenhower to meet with Faubus to work out a settlement, and over Brownell's protest — the attorney general was sure Faubus was more interested in reelection than in compromise — Eisenhower agreed. The meeting was held at the president's vacation house in Newport, Rhode Island, on September 14, with the TV networks alerted and the nation watching and waiting.

No official record of the one-on-one conversation exists but afterward, in the presence of Brownell, Faubus, and others, Eisenhower said he and Faubus had agreed that the black children would be admitted to Central High. Faubus did not dispute this statement. Later, in a diary entry of October 8, the president recounted that he had proposed that Faubus leave the Guard in place to preserve public discipline but change its orders to let Guardsmen escort the black children into the school. Eisenhower would then instruct the Justice Department not to seek a contempt order. The president told his diary that he had assured Faubus that he did not want "to see any governor humiliated" and in return "got definitely the understanding" that Faubus would revoke his order to the Guard to keep the blacks out of Central High.[3]

If there was such an understanding, Faubus did not keep his side of the bargain. Instead, he returned to Little Rock, issued a statement of defiance, and failed to appear in federal court on September 20, as ordered. That evening, in a statewide television speech, the governor announced that he was removing the National Guard. The next day, a threatening mob — partially from out of state — did materialize at Central High. Local police could not keep order and refused to escort the black children into school; the few youngsters who managed to get in were quickly mobbed and ousted by white students.

Mayor W. W. Mann and FBI agents on the scene, with the Constitution clearly being defied, then appealed for federal troops. In Washington, Brownell phoned the president to say flatly that Eisenhower had both the constitutional power and the duty to enforce the law. His meaning was clear: the time for news conference evasions was over.

On the phone from Newport, Eisenhower repeated to Brownell his familiar dictum: "If you have to use force, use overwhelming force, and save lives thereby," then finally acted on that premise. The very next morning, the men of the 101st Airborne Division (which had crowd-control experience) marched in battle array along Little Rock's streets, to surround Central High. Eisenhower also cut off Faubus's command of the Arkansas National Guard by calling it into federal service.

Thus, he decisively and once-and-for-all removed any remaining question whether he would enforce court orders and Supreme Court decisions — but even then, in a national television address, he held out the olive branch to his southern constituents, "the overwhelming majority" of southerners who were, he said, "united in their efforts to preserve and respect the law even when they disagree with it."

Deeds speak louder than words, however, and reaction in Congress was hostile and explosive. Among the most severe critics, predictably, was Richard Russell, who compared Eisenhower's actions to those of Hitler; less predictably, Senators John F. Kennedy and Lyndon B. Johnson also deplored the president's use of military force. JFK could not have known that in 1963, at the University of Mississippi, he would face much the same problem that confronted Eisenhower in Little Rock.[4]

The mob scenes from Little Rock had scarcely faded from the nation's television screens when, on October 4, 1957, the Soviet Union shocked Eisenhower, the administration, and the public by launching into space orbit the first man-made satellite. Since World War II, Americans in their vast power and prosperity had been accustomed to being number one in all fields, certainly including education and technology; even the threat of the Cold War had not dampened their economic, military, and political self-confidence — which many at home and abroad considered arrogance.

The Soviet satellite (*Sputnik*, or "traveling companion"), though unarmed and carrying no scientific equipment, shattered that complacency. Americans were stunned that the Russians, not they, had accomplished such a feat. And for the first time of any consequence, the national father figure often was blamed; he had held down spending it was said, especially by Democrats, had sought a balanced budget at the expense of national needs, neglected education, focused on missiles and bombs rather than on space, and his leadership generally had lulled the nation into a self-satisfaction that Eisenhower had encouraged and, in fact, personified.

Lampooning the president's well-known love of golf, for instance, the cartoonist of the *Nashville Tennessean*, Tom Little, pictured *Sputnik* high above the earth — followed by a golf ball.[5] More seriously, the scientist Edward Teller suggested that *Sputnik* was a greater American defeat than Pearl Harbor had been. The army and navy seized the moment to renew rivalry, the army claiming its Redstone missile could have launched an American satellite. Instead, the Eisenhower administration had assigned the program to the navy's Vanguard missile, which had flunked the job. And suddenly, with the success of *Sputnik*, the Soviets seemed not only hostile but formidable — ahead of the United States in space, perhaps in intercontinental missiles, even in science generally.

At the president's first news conference after *Sputnik,* the press was more demanding than it had ever been. Eisenhower assured the reporters and the nation that he saw nothing "significant in [*Sputnik*] as far as security is concerned." Even from him, that sounded like whistling past the graveyard, and the uproar of alarm and concern continued. As one result, Eisenhower consulted a broader range of scientists than had been his custom, then appointed Dr. James R. Killian of the Massachusetts Institute of Technology to a new position as his "science adviser" (actually, chairman of a President's Science Advisory Committee).

If *Sputnik* demanded anything, Americans of all persuasions and both parties seemed to believe, it was more spending — on education, science, space, research, military forces, fallout shelters, federal aid to this and federal support for that, including every congressman's favorite project for his district — an air base here, a missile site there. What should it profit the country to balance its budget, critics asked, but to lose its commanding position among other nations?

Unfortunately for most of the suppli-cants for funds, 1957 was a recession year, federal revenues were down, and the White House was occupied by a man who, if a father figure, was also a fiscal conservative who deplored deficit spending and believed he had a superior knowledge, particularly of military requirements, but also of other national needs. In the face of what was essentially a national panic, Eisenhower stayed calm, stood fast, refused to go into an emergency mode that would have spread the public fever even further and faster.[6] In that traumatic fall of 1957, he earned the title of "father figure," for as the nation clamored for action — almost any action! — the president's great prestige, experience, unperturbed attitude, and Americans' bedrock confidence in him (only momentarily shaken, if at all) was a necessary calming force. He said, in effect, that there was no need to panic, and events proved him right.

Sputnik was nevertheless an unwelcome turning point for the Eisenhower administration. The consequent public concern gave the president's critics newer and firmer ground for attacking him, and their criticisms came more often and more harshly. Together with an economic downturn and a new health problem, the new and less favorable atmosphere caused

Eisenhower and his administration to become more negative, more inward-looking — with unhappy consequences particularly for Richard Nixon, the Republican presidential candidate in 1960.[7]

On November 25, with *Sputnik* still a grim presence in the headlines and in Eisenhower's consciousness, he suffered a minor stroke while working at his desk in the Oval Office. Minor, of course, is a hindsight word; at the time, with Jim Hagerty's full-disclosure health policy still in force, that the president had suffered a stroke of any kind was front-page news — news that, coming on top of the 1955 heart attack, reenforced a major criticism *Sputnik* had renewed, roughly the same view I had tried to convince Mrs. Hoyt about during the 1956 election — that Eisenhower's health was too precarious for him to be running the country. In November 1957, moreover, he was sixty-seven years old.

Nevertheless, the stroke was minor, only temporarily affecting the president's speech; it was a bad public relations blow but physically only a "spasm" in a minor capillary. Soon after the president was stricken, Nixon had had to fill in for him at a state dinner, but quickly, Eisenhower's speech began to clear up. Two days after the afternoon stroke, he and Mamie drove to Gettysburg, and by mid-December — with his speech virtually unaffected — he was able to attend NATO meetings in Europe and to engage in important talks about a nuclear test ban: the old Adlai Stevenson proposal that refused to die, despite Eisenhower's campaign derision.[8]

Nor did there seem to be any end to public and congressional demands for more spending — particularly more defense spending, triggered by public fear that if the Soviets were ahead in satellites, they might also be ahead in missiles. Eisenhower doubted that and anyway believed that in defense "enough is enough." As 1958 developed, he had to reject supposedly irresistible demands for more B-52 bombers (if the six hundred on hand weren't sufficient, he said, seven hundred would be no better), for a nuclear aircraft carrier, for nuclear- or atomic-powered aircraft, a nuclear-propelled satellite, a nuclear-powered rocket trip to the moon, and for more personnel in all three armed services (as to the latter, he noted rather acidly that no Marines had taken part in his D-Day landings).

The administration's attempt to catch up to *Sputnik* (driven more by competitive political pressures than by any military necessity that Eisenhower ever conceded) went badly; a Vanguard rocket caught fire while trying to launch a satellite in late 1957, and when *Explorer I* did go up in January 1958, it weighed only 39 pounds. A successor, launched by a Vanguard in March, weighed a mere three pounds. As if to "rub it in," *Sputnik II* tipped the scales at 3,000 pounds when the Soviets launched it in May.

One useful result of these satellite embarrassments was the National Aeronautics and Space Agency — to the establishment of which Eisenhower only reluctantly agreed, fearing wrongly that NASA would give undue priority to satellite over missile development. The new agency would control all space activities save those "primarily associated with national defense."

A less important matter caused Eisenhower even more trouble and, he claimed, great personal regret: charges that Chief of Staff Sherman Adams had done and accepted favors for and from one Bernard Goldfine, another New Englander, who was having problems with the Securities

Exchange Commission. A frosty Yankee known as Eisenhower's "Abominable No Man," Adams was not really liked by anyone (save perhaps the president himself, who had had to deal with him), and almost everyone, particularly Democrats and liberals, blamed him (usually erroneously) for any and everything they didn't like about Eisenhower or the administration. In fact, Adams was a flintily efficient bureaucrat and White House manager who had no time for pleasantries and little influence on the president's policies.

A Democratic subcommittee of the House charged that Goldfine had paid some of Adams's hotel bills in Boston and that in return Adams had interceded for Goldfine with the SEC. In a subcommittee hearing, Adams admitted — voluntarily, not under subpoena — a lack of "prudence" about the hotel bills but denied giving Goldfine any help other than a single phone call asking the SEC to speed up its investigation. Eisenhower himself saw nothing wrong with accepting gifts — like the cattle for his Gettysburg farm, or "Mamie's Cottage" at the Augusta golf course — and thought the charges politically inspired. He defended his staff chief and incautiously told a news conference, "I need him." The remark delighted and seemed to vindicate those who charged that Eisenhower was too ill or too old, or both, to be president.

More Goldfine gifts — including a vicuna coat — then were disclosed. Republicans, who liked Adams no better than anyone did, and who knew the 1958 midterm elections were approaching, joined the mob calling for his political blood. Recognizing a crisis, Eisenhower fell back on his traditional "prat boy" system: he sent Richard Nixon to tell Adams that he had become a political liability. Nixon laid it on: if the coming elections went badly for the Republicans, he warned, Adams would be blamed. Adams calmly replied that if Eisenhower wanted him to quit, Eisenhower should tell him so to his face.

As the election neared, Republican chances — even given Eisenhower's continuing, if diminished, personal popularity — began to look hopeless. A party and a president perhaps in power too long, Little Rock, *Sputnik*, an economic slump in the early part of the year, the president's rejection of various spending proposals, a vigorous Democratic campaign centered on the false charge that Eisenhower had let the Soviets forge ahead in missiles, and —

not least — the sensational case of Sherman Adams: all seemed to foretell a smashing Republican defeat. So, by September, *Republican*, not just Democratic, demands for Adams's head were piling up in the White House.

Even Eisenhower saw that Adams had to go, so again he called on a prat boy. This time Meade Alcorn, the Republican national chairman, was asked to join Nixon in talking to Adams. Nixon ducked out, but Alcorn finally got the message across — though the granite-faced Adams still demanded to hear the bad news from Eisenhower personally. "Miffed" at Nixon's evasion and feeling "used," Alcorn later told William Ewald that "this was the only time in my three years in Washington that I wished I'd never heard of the Republican National Committee. This was the one time when I thought the President might have done it himself."[9]

He and Adams had forced Eisenhower's hand, however, and the president met with his chief of staff on September 17 to tell him — as six years before during the fund crisis, and two years earlier when he had hoped to dump the vice president, he had told Nixon: "You will have to take the initiative yourself." Adams agreed to resign but, a tough customer to the end, he also requested a month's delay to put White House administrative affairs in order. Eisenhower consented, then an hour later — realizing that a month would cover the late stages of the campaign — called Adams back to say that he had to go at once.

Adams did, on September 22, too late to save Eisenhower and the Republican Party — Nixon carrying the campaign load — from devastating defeat on November 4. The GOP was reduced that day in 1958 to about a two-to-one minority in both houses of Congress and could win or retain only fourteen of the fifty state governorships; Eisenhower would have to work with a third consecutive Congress controlled by the opposition. Even Minority Leader William Knowland, sometimes known as "the senator from Formosa," who had recklessly decided to run for governor of California, suffered smashing defeat by that state's Democratic attorney general, Edmund G. "Pat" Brown.

The one Republican bright spot in November 1958 — Nelson Rockefeller's election as governor of New York — was small consolation to Dwight Eisenhower. By 1958 he had little use for a former

White House assistant who was entirely too independent for the taste of a man used to being commander in chief.

Eight

Months earlier, in January 1958, Egypt and Syria, in the wake of the European-Israeli attack on the Suez Canal, had formed an unusual international union — the United Arab Republic. Jordan and Iraq, both feudal monarchies, responded with another hybrid federation, the Arab Union. The Soviets were sending military equipment to the UAR, the United States was arming and equipping the AU, Saudi Arabia, and Lebanon, and the French were supplying Israel. As if the Middle East had not been troublesome enough all along, suddenly an arms race was flourishing in the region.

Perhaps again using what Fred Greenstein called his "hidden-hand" method, Eisenhower expressed public concern about Middle Eastern Communism, of which actually there was very little; his real worry was Arab nationalism. The UAR, for instance, under the leadership of the persistent Nasser, was openly inviting other anti-Israel nations to join, and the Soviet Union was arming the UAR. In the heart of the Cold War, Washington was sure to regard these developments with foreboding: suppose Israel should be crushed and the Soviets should get a stranglehold on Middle East oil?

On July 14, 1958, a pro-Nasser coup in Iraq, ending the Hashemite monarchy, heightened these fears, though Nasser himself was not known to be involved. King Saud demanded deployment of American troops in the Middle East — so that he would not have to join the UAR. President Camille Chamoun of Lebanon, fearing what had been Syria before it joined the UAR, also requested American intervention. Watching all this unhappily, Eisenhower called a meeting of his top advisers on July 15 but conceded in his memoirs that he already had decided to intervene, "specifically in Lebanon, to stop the trend toward chaos."[1]

"Foster," he told Dulles, who appeared to have recovered from his cancer operation, "I've already made up my mind. We're going in."[2]

Why would this differ from the previous year's British-French assault on Suez? Because, in the secretary of state's opinion, Chamoun had *invited* the United States to intervene. Still, Dulles warned, other nations in the region might be affronted by the presence of U.S. troops and could possibly threaten the West's oil supply.

Eisenhower had made his decision, however, and he was still a general used not only to command but to moving forces rapidly and with purpose. To avoid any possibility of resistance, he told the Pentagon to have U.S. Marines ashore in Lebanon by 9 P.M., Eastern Standard Time, that very night, with not even Chamoun given notice.[3] That afternoon, the president briefed unenthusiastic legislative leaders; Lodge was instructed to tell the Security Council that the United States sought only to stabilize the Middle East until the UN could take over the mission; and in a call to Harold Macmillan, an old Eisenhower friend and the new British prime minister (Eden having not long survived the Suez debacle), the president suggested a similar British intervention in Jordan, this time with U.S. logistical support.

The entire action ordered by Eisenhower basically was finished in less than a month. The Marines encountered no resistance in Lebanon or in securing the airfield and the capital, and U.S. forces refrained from operating elsewhere in the country. An unopposed British paratroop landing in Jordan on July 22 bolstered the local regime. Khrushchev called for a summit meeting, but otherwise — even after Nasser flew to Moscow to seek aid — the Soviets took no action. The Marines began to withdraw in August and the last American forces were out of Lebanon by October 25.

Eisenhower had hit several birds with one impressive stone. He had given Nasser a good look at U.S. strength and flexibility, in the process showing up the Soviets as an unreliable source of aid. He had demonstrated to the Democrats and the public that the New Look in defense was not too muscle-bound — or Eisenhower himself too old and weak — to respond appropriately to challenges anywhere in the world. The immediate situation in the Middle East had been stabilized without provoking war. And the threat to Western oil supplies that Foster Dulles feared had not arisen.

The Democrats were not chastened, however — or not for long. They fiercely criticized the Lebanon intervention and never let up in their "missile gap" charges.[4] The substantial payoff came for them, as we have seen, in the November 1958 elections.

On New Year's Day 1959, a new political weapon fell into opposition hands: Fidel Castro led his Cuban rebels in triumph into Havana, and Fulgencio Batista, a corrupt dictator but a staunch U.S. ally, ran for safety. Having little choice, the Eisenhower administration figuratively held its nose and recognized the Castro regime; but by mid-February, when Castro took over personally as premier, the new Cuban government had shown itself, if revolutionary, also repressive and incipiently anti-American. Castro had executed several Batista supporters; worse, as Washington saw things, he had recognized the Communist Party of Cuba.

How could this happen, the Democrats and other critics demanded, only ninety miles from Florida? How could Communism have penetrated almost to American shores? Many Americans were outraged and most sympathized with Governor George Wallace of Alabama, who professed to have known all along that Castro himself was a Communist. How could the Eisenhower administration not have perceived the same thing?

When the young Cuban leader visited

Washington, Eisenhower, in an egregious snub, shunted him off to Nixon, who recognized Castro as an "outright Communist."[5] Nevertheless, Nixon told the president that "because [Castro] has the power to lead . . . we have no choice but to try to orient him in the right direction."

Eisenhower ignored this prescient advice and listened to the CIA instead, despite certain qualms about Allen Dulles. The president thought Dulles "with all his limitations" was the best man to run the intelligence agency, a post in which the president believed "a strange kind of genius" was needed. When in 1960 Dulles proposed a plan for sabotaging a Cuban sugar refinery, the president replied a little testily: "Instead of this one-shot action, Allen, why don't you come back with a comprehensive program?"

The old taste for covert action, successful in Iran and Guatemala, clearly was still alive in the man of peace. One result of this and other Eisenhower suggestions to the CIA — and the agency's to him — was a Nicaraguan training camp for a band of Cuban fighting men hostile to Castro and financed by the CIA. This force was never actually deployed by Eisenhower, but it was there to be used when the Kennedy administration took office in 1961, keeping Allen Dulles briefly in charge of the CIA.[6]

Most of the Cuban fighters subsequently were killed or captured during the ill-fated Bay of Pigs invasion that Kennedy ordered but only halfheartedly supported. Allen Dulles later told me that he had forced Kennedy's hand by asking him, "Are you going to be less anti-Communist than Eisenhower?"

A more daunting problem arose in Europe owing to Khrushchev's blustery demands for a peace treaty with East Germany, which, the Soviet leader contended, would put an end to Allied occupation rights in divided Berlin. He set a deadline of May 27, 1959, at which time, he said, he would sign such a treaty even if the Allies didn't. After that, since the Allies would have no treaty with East Germany, they would have to use force to gain access to Berlin (located deep within East Germany).

Eisenhower insisted, in response, that Allied occupation rights rested on the wartime Yalta agreements and were in no way affected by the status of East Germany. He believed Khrushchev was bluffing in order to force a summit meeting on Berlin. But the net effect of the Soviet leader's big talk was to increase the U.S. public's fears of another war and to intensify demands from the Democrats — aided and abetted by Pentagon, military, and defense industry officials — for more spending on more planes and missiles and men. As May 27 neared, a war scare swept the country.

Air Force Chief of Staff Twining declared himself and his service ready to fight a "general nuclear war," but the president refused to authorize the use of armed force. Eisenhower went no further than to say that if after May 27 the Soviets stopped any U.S. vehicle on the way to Berlin, he would order an airlift into that city, break relations with the Soviet Union, take the matter to the UN, and prepare for general war.

Otherwise, he steadfastly denied war was impending, or that there even was a crisis. To Congress, the press, the Joint Chiefs, even to some in his own administration, he counseled — as so often before — patience, calm, common sense. Khrushchev wanted to scare the nation into over-reaction, ultimately into overspending and bankruptcy, the president insisted. Against relentless pressures from the Joint Chiefs and even his own defense secretary — by then, Neil McElroy — he stood fast against building the expensive B-70 bomber, which he believed was unneeded in the missile age. And even though he had no intention of giving in to Soviet demands, he signaled across the Iron Curtain that he might be willing to negotiate on the status of Berlin, if the talks also covered German reunification.

In all these ways, Eisenhower once again, as if he were the head of a threatened family, justified his standing as a father figure — but in 1959, as it often seemed, to no avail. He also reminded reporters at a news conference — the means by which he had so frequently attempted to lead — that he had not declared "nuclear war . . . a complete impossibility." (Let Khrushchev brood on that one.) But on April 13, as a meeting of foreign ministers resumed desultory test ban talks in Geneva, the president also wrote the Soviet premier that the United States no longer demanded a comprehensive nuclear test ban but would consider a prohibition of atmospheric tests, requiring only a simpler verification system. The carrot thus was extended with the stick.

In this delicate international period,

John Foster Dulles — hospitalized by a recurrence of cancer — died on May 24, 1959. Eisenhower was strongly affected; Dulles, though often disagreeing with him, had served the administration faithfully and well. He had mellowed even in his anti-Communist and hawkish views, particularly after he had seen that economic, not military, power had been most effective in the Suez crisis of 1956 (and perhaps in awareness of his own mortality). The president had come to hold Dulles in deep respect (though the two men were never close socially).

On May 27, 1959, the world's foreign ministers gathered in Washington to attend Dulles's funeral. Eisenhower invited them to lunch at the White House — not to gloat publicly at the relatively uneventful passage of Khrushchev's original deadline for an East German treaty, but with a sense of satisfaction, it may be imagined, that another Cold War challenge had been survived without war or surrender, or even a damaging jolt to the budget. Not least because he had again preserved the peace, he was rewarded with a jump in his Gallup poll standing from 49 percent in the post-*Sputnik* period to 66 percent in late 1959.

★ ★ ★

The lumbering old four-engine *Columbine* was replaced in 1959 by a sleek new jet transport, designated *Air Force One*, as the president's personal aircraft. To break it in, and for other more pressing reasons, Eisenhower decided that summer to visit the major Western European capitals. The result, while diplomatically useful, was primarily to demonstrate the enduring popularity of the conquering hero of World War II and the subsequent man of peace. Welcoming crowds were enormous and warm, old friendships with men like Macmillan were revived, talks with iron personalities like Konrad Adenauer and Charles de Gaulle were cordial, and the president took a brief vacation at a castle to which the Scottish people had given him lifetime possession. In London in a television appearance with Macmillan, Eisenhower got off one of the remarks for which he is best remembered, or should be: "I think the people want peace so much that one of these days governments had better get out of the way and let them have it."[7]

Back in Washington in September, the president got ready for one of the most unprecedented, unexpected, and controversial events of his years in office — a visit by Soviet Premier Khrushchev. Eisenhower believed, in a general sort of way, that obtaining a real, long-term peace would require such a high-level meeting, though he had no specific diplomatic agenda. To associates he did remark, presumably in jest, that if Khrushchev were to threaten war, Eisenhower "would immediately call his bluff and ask him to agree on a day to start."[8]

He also said he wanted the Soviet visitor to see a happy people and all the material progress they had made and maintained in a free country, under a democratic system. No doubt he also felt, as most leaders in most countries have, that if he could only sit down in private with an opponent, they could settle peacefully whatever divided them. The two men did agree that neither wanted war, though on most specific issues they held to their fixed positions.

Khrushchev's campaign-style tour of the country — including a movie set in Hollywood and a midwestern farm — was spectacular and recorded every step of the way by a huge American and a small Russian press corps. The Soviet premier proved to be a colorful and vigorous man; as someone said, the sort of politician who, shorn of his nationality and ideology, might well have been a big winner in an American election.[9] Clearly, he was a man who knew and coveted the value of headlines and was willing to make them in a variety of ways — angrily, humorously, derisively, sometimes threateningly, as in a speech at the National Press Club when he said memorably, "We will bury you."

Khrushchev was not, however, as impressed as Eisenhower had hoped with American affluence — the abundance of automobiles, roads, and private houses that he could see from helicopter rides. Waste, he snorted. And though he repeatedly stressed his interest in disarmament, he balanced that with copious boasts about Soviet missiles, submarines, and military prowess generally. But he did not return to the dicey Berlin question, and the two leaders were able to agree on a summit meeting in Paris in May, to discuss — at last — a nuclear test ban. After that, the Eisenhower family would visit Russia in another Cold War milestone.

In fiscal 1959 — which ran from July 1, 1958, to June 30, 1959 — a sluggish economy and various spending increases had caused the Eisenhower administration and Congress, to the president's displeasure, to run up a budget deficit of nearly $13 billion. A major factor was the economic slump that caused federal revenues to fall in calendar 1957 and the early part of 1958. In the spring of the latter year, however, things turned around and the economy began to expand.

Eisenhower the fiscal conservative and his equally conservative advisers — Treasury Secretary Robert Anderson and Raymond Saulnier, the chairman of the Council of Economic Advisers — either did not notice the pickup or, following their economic ideology instead of fiscal pragmatism, misinterpreted its meaning and effect.[10] In January 1959, not least because Eisenhower believed the Democrats' triumph in the November 1958 election had filled Congress with "people that I would class among the spenders," they sent up a budget for fiscal 1960 that, if adopted, would result in a $100 million surplus.

Neither for the first nor the last time, Eisenhower had misjudged the Democrats. In 1959, rather than being profligate spenders, they decided to outdo the president in reducing federal expenditures. By the time the two congressional parties were done leap-frogging over each other in ever bigger spending cuts, the fiscal 1960 budget they adopted featured a *$269 million* surplus. That may have pleased the White House but the inescapable economic fact was that such a dramatic one-year swing in federal spending — from a $13 billion deficit to a nearly $300 million surplus — virtually strangled the economic recovery that had begun in April 1958.

In 1959, moreover, the Federal Reserve, which had been ritually keeping money tight since 1956, actually raised the crucial discount rate from 2.5 to 4 percent. Restrictive fiscal and monetary policy combined resulted in the shortest economic expansion of the postwar years, and in April 1960 the economy began sliding into a new recession, which was to last into 1961.

Eisenhower may not have seen this coming, but the politically minded Richard Nixon certainly did. In 1960, Nixon was preparing to run for president and one of his strongest supporters — Dr. Arthur Burns, who had preceded Saulnier as chairman of the Council of Economic Advisers — warned him that current economic policy would have the nation in recession just as the voters were making up their minds. But when Nixon urged a loosening of credit and higher defense spending — the latter a particular red flag to the president — the doctrinaire Eisenhower economic team paid no attention. Anderson and Saulnier were dead-set against what they considered a reckless approach and Eisenhower readily agreed with them.

In fact, they were condemning the vice president and the Republican Party to defeat in 1960. While the economic downturn and consequent rising unemployment were not alone the cause of Nixon's downfall in November 1960, economic recession was prominent among the many factors that gave John F. Kennedy his razor-thin victory.[11]

In 1960, Eisenhower held Kennedy, the "young whippersnapper," in contempt and believed Kennedy's election to the presidency would be a repudiation of his own eight-year record. So his politically obtuse economic policy in 1959 and 1960 does not seem to have been a deliberate attempt to sabotage Nixon. Still, in view of the president's reluctant acceptance of Nixon as a running mate in 1956 and as his successor at the top of the Republican ticket or in the White House in 1960, and of the less-than-all-out support he extended to the vice president before and during the

1960 campaign, as well as his repeated efforts in both years to find someone to take Nixon's place — in view of all this, it's fair enough to wonder whether Eisenhower's conviction that no other man was as suited as he to world leadership, or could do his job as well, was reflected subconsciously in his overt actions in that final year.

William Ewald seems to have touched on the truth as closely as anyone could have: "The plain fact was that Eisenhower did not so . . . unqualifiedly favor Nixon — especially now that Nixon was moving to replace him at the apex of government — that he would sacrifice his own self-definition . . . in order to help him. . . . Eisenhower did not so much wish victory for Nixon as he wished defeat for Kennedy."[12]

Nine

Vice President Richard M. Nixon was not only the logical but the preferred choice of the Republican Party for its presidential nomination in 1960. Dwight Eisenhower may never have realized (or if he did, he may secretly have resented) the high standing Nixon had achieved within the party owing to his early fame as a Red-hunter, his later role as a bridge between Eisenhower Republicans and the Old Guard, his yeoman work in congressional relations and other political chores during the 1950s, and his assiduous cultivation — as he traveled the country in the political campaigns of 1952, '54, '56, '58, and in between — of every state, county, and local party leader he could reach, as well as party bigwigs like Tom Dewey and Styles Bridges.

Even if an aloof Eisenhower did not know or acknowledge it, Richard Nixon by 1960 was easily the number two man in the Republican Party (number one on some scorecards) and its natural presidential nominee, self- and party-promoted as vastly experienced in national and world affairs and a sort of "assistant president" in the Eisenhower administration. In fact, Nixon never had played such a role, nor had Eisenhower even considered him for it, but the puffery seemed plausible for a vice president, particularly to Republican Nixon fans.

The vice president entered 1960, moreover, in a blaze of perhaps peculiar glory — derived from a hostile reception in 1959 on his tour of South America, during which he and his wife had been so threatened that Eisenhower had sent the Marines to extricate them; and from his "kitchen debate" with Khrushchev in Moscow, in which he had managed to thrust his forefinger into Khrushchev's chest, a priceless political scene captured for American distribution by an Associated Press photographer. What could be more attractive to the voters than "standing up" to foreign mobs and telling off the boss Communist? Nixon in Moscow, said *Time* magazine, had been "the personification of a kind of disciplined vigor that belie[s] tales of the decadent and limp-wristed West." By November 1959, Nixon had even come from behind to lead John F. Kennedy, the likely candidate of the majority Democrats, by 53 to 47 in the Gallup poll.

His only conceivable rival for the presidential nomination was Nelson Rockefeller, who had won the governorship of New York in the otherwise dismal (for Republicans) election of 1958. At one point, Eisenhower — never comfortable with the idea of Nixon as president — even proposed to an associate a wild scheme hatched by a speechwriter, Malcolm Moos: Rockefeller should take second place on Nixon's ticket, with the understanding that after one term Nixon would step down and Rockefeller could run for president. It need hardly be said that this idea went nowhere, particularly with Nixon and Rockefeller.

As the year wore on, Rockefeller proved not as sure-footed in national politics as he was in New York; he failed to wage a serious national campaign, and when the GOP national convention opened in Chicago in July 1960, Nixon's nomination, never in any real doubt, was a "sure thing." But Rockefeller had been calling loudly for greater defense spending, and from Chicago, Nixon — apparently under the impression that he needed to lock up the governor's support — flew to New York and joined Rockefeller in what the press called the "Pact of Fifth Avenue."

For once, Nixon's acute political antennae had failed to vibrate. The agreement called, among other things, for "increased expenditures" for the military — thereby repudiating not only Eisenhower administration policy but the hero of World War II himself. Eisenhower was outraged by the "Pact," as he had already been by Rockefeller's temerity in challenging the master; so, still officially in charge, the president forced Nixon to keep the New York statement out of the Republican platform. Nixon did, was duly nominated anyway, chose Henry Cabot Lodge as his running mate, and proceeded to the campaign.[1] But Eisenhower's already dubious view of his young vice president may never have recovered from this early affront.

At any rate, at his news conference on August 24, when asked to give an example of Nixon's influence on administration policy, Eisenhower replied that Nixon took "a full part" in all discussions but that the president alone made the final decisions. The questioner persisted: Could Eisenhower give "an example of a major idea" of Nixon's? For whatever reason, the president seemed to have had enough: "If you give me a week I might think of one," he snapped. "I don't remember."

The president thus delivered a torpedo below the waterline to the Nixon campaign theme of "experience" by an "assistant president." Soon after the news conference, realizing his gaffe (if that's what it was), he called Nixon to apologize, but the remark already had entered the ample file of Nixoniana, never to be expunged. What damage had been done to the vice president's immediate campaign can't be measured, but it may well have been substantial; nor can it be known what new degree of resentment an insecure Nixon may have stored away among the many he brooded upon.

The story of the Kennedy-Nixon campaign of 1960 — the closest presidential election in history until then, and the first to feature televised debates between the candidates — needs no retelling. But it does need to be said in a book about President Eisenhower that, at the time, few election analysts or journalists doubted that, had he been constitutionally eligible, he could easily have defeated either Kennedy or Nixon and won a third term — despite his age and health and eight years already in office. And though the corollary proposition is by no means so certain, it's reasonable to suppose that Eisenhower might also have put Nixon over the top — despite the economy, despite the president's lack of enthusiasm, despite the devastating "give me a week" remark.

That Eisenhower ultimately did not do so (which doesn't prove that he couldn't have) was not his fault; rather, it was the deliberate decision of Richard Nixon, who failed — for whatever reason — to use the president to best effect in a long, close, hard-fought campaign. Close observers of the embittered Nixon can hardly doubt that he kept Eisenhower too far on the sidelines because *he,* Nixon, wanted and needed the credit for victory — he alone. In this view, Nixon did not want it said that he had won only because of Eisenhower's strong voice and great national standing; eight years of playing second fiddle, of not being sufficiently mature, were enough.

After Eisenhower's death, in Nixon's second memoir, *RN,* he put forward a self-exculpating explanation. Both Mamie Eisenhower and Dr. Snyder had importuned him to keep the president's campaigning to a minimum, Nixon disclosed, to avoid strain on Eisenhower's heart, and he complied. This can't be verified, since Dr. Snyder had died before *RN* came out, and Mamie Eisenhower soon after. But Snyder and Mamie had wanted Eisenhower to run in 1956, soon after his heart attack, as better therapy than retirement. Why should they have thought, four years later, that a few campaign trips and speeches would have been too much for the president's heart?

Whatever explanation one accepts, William Ewald describes a White House luncheon on October 31, 1960, when Eisenhower entertained Nixon, Hagerty, Republican National Chairman Len Hall, and a team of speechwriters. At the table, the president told Nixon that he and Hall had agreed to expand Eisenhower's speaking schedule in the final week, to include New York, downstate Illinois, and Michigan. Nixon refused the offer, not only at first but after the president insisted.

His attitude angered the short-fused Eisenhower. Pointing to Nixon as they left the luncheon, he said to Malcolm Moos: "He doesn't even walk like a president."[2] And he later told Hall: "Goddamnit, he looks like a loser to me."[3]

In the event, Nixon *was* a loser — just

barely — but it's permissible speculation to wonder whether he would have been a winner had he let the most popular man in America, one of the best-loved presidents in history, make the Republican case in three vital states in that last week of a campaign ultimately lost by only about a hundred thousand votes out of more than sixty million cast.

Much as he desired Republican victory to vindicate his own administration and to keep the government out of the hands of "spenders" and that "young whipper-snapper" from Massachusetts, President Eisenhower had greater concerns in 1960 than the election — among them the nuclear test ban first proposed by Adlai Stevenson in 1956.

The idea had won increasing worldwide acceptance after that, and a test ban became a major second-term issue for Eisenhower — who might himself have proposed such a step if Stevenson hadn't done it first. In December 1957, Nikolai Bulganin — clinging to some semblance of power in Moscow — grabbed the initiative for the Soviets by proposing a two- or three-year moratorium on nuclear tests. In January 1958, the president replied that he could agree if the moratorium were linked to an ultimate end to nuclear weapons production. The Soviets then said no, and showed their insincerity by proceeding with an extensive series of tests. When the series was concluded, on March 31, Khrushchev (by then in full power) announced that Moscow was unilaterally halting all future tests — a shrewd and cost-free move, since he knew the United States was even then preparing for a test series and that the Soviet Union could not be ready for another for some time.

After *Sputnik* went up in 1957, Eisenhower had appointed a Scientific Advisory Committee headed by Dr. James Killian of MIT. In April 1958 the committee announced that in a review of nuclear policy its technical experts had concluded that an inspection system could be devised to detect underground nuclear explosions with as little power as the equivalent of two kilotons of TNT. With that report in hand, Eisenhower, at Foster Dulles's instigation, wrote Khrushchev to propose talks on the technicalities of inspection as a preliminary to "putting political decisions into effect" — a basic change in American policy from linkage of a test ban to an end to nuclear weapons production.

When Khruschchev accepted the new proposal, the way was clear for serious Soviet-American test-ban negotiations — as opposed to posturing on both sides — although major figures among Eisenhower's advisers, including Defense Secretary McElroy, AEC Chairman John McCone, and his predecessor, Lewis Strauss, were opposed. No doubt there was disagreement in Moscow, too. But by mid-August, both sides' technical experts, meeting in Geneva, had concluded that an effective inspection system was "feasible"; they differed only on the number of control posts needed. On August 22, therefore, Eisenhower offered to begin test-ban negotiations with the Soviet Union, starting October 31, 1958.

From within the administration and without a chorus of protests erupted, and McCone promptly demanded "one more test" — which ultimately was to become a series of nineteen explosions. Annnoyed, but aware of dissent even within the scientific community, Eisenhower reluctantly agreed. Predictably, the same last-minute maneuverings went on in Moscow; Khrushchev agreed to the October 31 talks but had to allow fourteen more test explosions — larger and with more fallout than those of the United States. Altogether in 1958, the two superpowers set off eighty-one nuclear explosions, to a rising world-wide tide of complaints about fallout, before getting down to the complicated business of agreeing on a test ban.

The Geneva talks, however, quickly bogged down on the issue whether to focus on a comprehensive test ban, as the Soviets wanted, or the details of an inspection system, as the United States insisted. Ultimately, Moscow yielded and the conferees settled on an inspection system requiring 180 control posts. That was no sooner settled than they deadlocked on a Soviet demand for a veto in the contemplated seven-nation control commission. To make matters worse, back in the United States, Eisenhower's Science Advisory Committee reneged on its earlier report on inspection, telling the president that the experts had decided they could not detect under-ground explosions of less than twenty kilo-tons — a standard that would demand thousands of control posts. But in Geneva, the Russians would not even talk about expansion of a system to which they already had agreed.

Taking a great political risk — in the view of many "experts," a national security risk as well — Eisenhower then announced a unilateral U.S. moratorium on atmospheric tests — those most feared for their radioactive fallout.[4] After the testing excesses of 1958, this move gained worldwide acclaim and forced the Soviets to follow suit — meaning that both sides would test only underground, with no atmospheric fallout. To the consternation of hawks within and without the administration, Eisenhower had stopped testing in the atmosphere with no inspection system in place, without any reciprocal concession from Moscow, and with no guarantee, save faith and world opinion, that the Soviets would comply. But they did, and on April 13, 1959, Eisenhower could and did go further: he wrote Khrushchev that the United States was willing to talk about a "limited" — or atmospheric — test ban that would not require a complex and invasive inspection system.

Even so, no real progress was made at Geneva for the rest of 1959. In that year and in 1960, Eisenhower was fighting doggedly, and usually winning, in major battles against his own Defense Department and Joint Chiefs of Staff, who sometimes were aided and abetted by the Democrats in Congress, and often by the press. All wanted more "defense" and relentlessly pressed the case — for instance — for the B-70 bomber — at the same time that they wanted more nuclear missiles. Eisenhower's essential argument, besides his known military expertise, was that "enough is enough"; he believed the United States already had enough weapons to destroy the Soviet Union several times over. The U.S. stockpile of nuclear weapons, he estimated, numbered five to seven thousand; and at one point, he wondered aloud what might happen to the Northern Hemisphere if all that megatonnage were exploded.[5] What, he asked, could possibly be done with more?

In these bureaucratic battles, Eisenhower usually managed to hold the line on spending and on additional "defense," but as we have seen, his budgetary policy was about to precipitate an economic downturn. He remained determined to get a test-ban treaty, which had become one of his major goals, and he was irritated by the deadlock in Geneva. Therefore, he announced to the world that the moratorium being observed by the United States would come to an end on December 31, 1959. After that the United States would not test without advance notice.

Khrushchev replied that the Soviets would not test again until the United States did. Apparently encouraged or at least more hopeful than ever, the president then took a plunge that probably neither he nor his hardest-line advisers ever had expected. On February 11, at a news conference — having come an infinite distance from Stevenson's "theatrical" idea of 1956 — Dwight Eisenhower announced that he could accept a treaty banning all nuclear tests in the atmosphere, in the oceans, in outer space, and underground that could be detected (in effect, underground tests over twenty kilotons of power).

Few events can have shown more effectively the power of presidential leadership in the American government. Had Eisenhower operated more collegially, or with a "war cabinet," or even with greater deference to associates, he probably could not have made such a far-reaching and radical proposal (in terms of Cold War and 1950s politics). His announcement was fought, and fiercely, by the military, the Atomic Energy Commission, many influential congressional and Democratic voices (particularly members of the Joint Committee on Atomic Energy), the intelligence community, hard-line journalists, and some leading scientists — notably Edward Teller and those on the AEC payroll. Even among all these important "nays," the president's "aye" — as Lincoln memorably noted — meant that "the ayes have it."

As Eisenhower had hoped, moreover, the Soviets — from their point of view — were equally forthcoming. They agreed to negotiations for such a treaty, which — if achieved — would result in the American inspection teams on their territory that they had steadily resisted, and they set only the minor condition that the United States accept a moratorium on small underground tests. To Eisenhower, as he told another news conference, that suggested that the Soviets, too, wanted "a degree of disarmament" and were willing "to stop testing."

That, of course, remained to be seen — obviously, at the summit. And it was not long before the president could tell the world that he, Prime Minister Macmillan, and President de Gaulle had agreed that the Paris summit scheduled in May 1959 would be devoted primarily to disarmament, including a verifiable test ban. Not in a decade of unremitting Cold War had prospects seemed more glowing for superpower agreement, and nuclear peace.

226

There matters stood until early April 1959, when Richard Bissell of the CIA asked the president to authorize another U-2 overflight of the Soviet Union. The bizarre, high-flying spy plane — a forerunner of today's camera-equipped satellites — had become a major Cold War weapon. Not only had it helped Eisenhower detect the budding crisis in the Middle East in 1956; its overflights of the Soviet Union had provided him with the necessary information to deny the Democrats' charge, widely echoed in the press, that his budgetary penury had allowed a "missile gap" to develop (meaning that the Soviets were ahead in missile production and deployment).[6]

Eisenhower knew, from high-resolution photographs taken by the U-2 in its numerous flights over the Soviet Union, that the charge was not true. Not only was there no "missile gap," but the actual balance of power was the other way around, with the United States fielding substantially more ICBMs than the Soviets had even produced.[7] The president denied the charge repeatedly and forcefully but not convincingly, because he believed the evidence he needed to prove his point could

not be disclosed. The U-2 was a secret —
though not entirely from the Soviets —
and Eisenhower could not prove his
denials without publicly admitting that the
United States was violating the airspace of
the Soviet Union, which would be an
international insult. Such an admission
also would violate the president's proven
taste for covert warfare.

The Soviets were "unofficially" aware of
the spy flights, but it was believed they
could do nothing to stop them. Even in the
unlikely event that they should shoot down
a U-2, the CIA assumed, they could not
tell the world without admitting that they
had been overflown and spied upon, perhaps for years — a humiliation they were
believed unlikely to invite. Eisenhower was
wary of this reasoning, since he knew that
if a U-2 should be lost within the Soviet
Union while the test-ban talks were
pending, U.S. sincerity in those talks
would be suspect, and his own reputation
for honesty diminished.

Nevertheless, when Bissell asked for
another flight in order to check on reports
of new Soviet missile sites, Eisenhower
incautiously authorized it for April 9. The
Soviets, as usual, fired surface-to-air missiles at the plane but the U-2 mission was

completed successfully — whereupon Bissell requested still another flight, and Eisenhower even more incautiously gave him a two-week window in which to launch it. Weather prevented high-level photography in that time period and Bissell requested an extension. Inexplicably, with the summit about to open, Eisenhower gave him another week, though specifying with prudence more apparent than real that no mission was to be undertaken after May 1.

Thus it was that on May 1, 1960, a U-2 piloted by Francis Gary Powers took off in clear weather from Adana, Turkey, for an espionage flight over the Soviet Union. That afternoon, when about 1,300 miles inside Russia, Powers reported an engine flameout — but after that, nothing was heard from him. For several days, however, from Eisenhower on down, there was little worry in Washington. After all, Powers had been instructed, if necessary, to destroy the plane and himself, and he had the means to do so. Khrushchev would not want to admit that his country could be so easily penetrated and spied upon; and in any case, there would be no evidence. Powers would see to that.

Unfortunately, on May 5, Khrushchev

did tell the world that the Soviet Union had shot down an American spy plane over its territory. In an angry speech to the Supreme Soviet, he excoriated the U.S. "militarists" he said were responsible for the mission — but rather pointedly did not blame Eisenhower. The president probably should have seized this opening with a high-minded statement claiming personal responsibility for "national security" flights made necessary because the Soviet Union was a closed and threatening society — and pointing out that the flights actually had served the cause of peace by proving that no missile gap existed. Such a statement would at least have been honest and would have bolstered Eisenhower's position in the United States and among its allies.

Believing Khrushchev could have no proof of his charges, however, and perhaps still hoping to keep the U-2 a secret, Eisenhower at first did nothing, then made the fatal error of trying a cover-up. He approved a statement implying that the plane the Soviets had shot down was on a weather mission over Turkey but apparently had strayed off its course and into the Soviet Union.

The next day, Khrushchev released a

photo of a wrecked airplane — *not* the U-2. So, apparently, he still had no evidence of espionage. Therefore, Eisenhower stuck to the false weather story, as Khrushchev apparently had anticipated. But on May 7, again shouting angrily to the Supreme Soviet, Khrushchev blew up the weather story in Washington's collective face, including that of Dwight D. Eisenhower. "Parts of the plane" had been captured and the pilot was "alive and kicking," Khrushchev declared. He had the spool of spy film, too — proof of espionage that the CIA had been sure would be destroyed in the wreckage. In fact, everything that the agency had believed could not possibly happen *had* happened — the wreckage of an actual U-2 in Soviet hands, the film captured, Powers alive in captivity.

Eisenhower, still calm personally but displaying more bad judgment, then tried a different cover-up. He ordered a statement denying that Powers had had any authorization at all to fly over the Soviet Union — an obviously implausible story that, not incidentally, concealed Eisenhower's personal responsibility. That satisfied no one, as it implied that the president had no control over his own administration; so still another tack was taken — a statement that

Powers's flight had been undertaken under a generalized order of the president issued early in his administration, when he had been trying to protect the United States against a surprise attack. This time, Eisenhower specifically ordered that he not be linked to the fatal Powers mission.

Nothing worked, save to confuse the nation and the world and to display a disarray in Washington unprecedented in the Eisenhower era. Khrushchev blustered and threatened but still refrained from accusing the president personally; Eisenhower momentarily considered resignation, but he quickly recovered, briefed congressional leaders, met the press as usual, remarked that the closed Soviet system made spying "a distasteful but vital necessity," and suggested rather incredibly that the outlook for the summit had not changed — "not decisively."[8] But of course it had.

The president flew to Paris on May 14 and learned that Khrushchev, who already had arrived in the City of Light, had given de Gaulle a written statement demanding that Eisenhower condemn and renounce U-2 flights generally and punish those responsible for the Powers mission. Obviously, he knew Eisenhower would do none of this, much less apologize; the U.S. side concluded, therefore, that the Soviet leader had decided, even before the summit opened, to sabotage it.

Why? He had seemed to accept that disarmament, specifically a test ban, was in the interest of the Soviet Union as well as of the United States. He himself had spy satellites crossing over the United States. The KGB was at least as active in espionage as the CIA, if not more so. The Soviet Union had been affronted, but not mortally wounded; and it seemed to Eisenhower, Macmillan, and de Gaulle — all old acquaintances from World War II, still united against a threatening foe — that Khrushchev was not only making a figurative mountain out of a relative mole hill, but that he was acting against his country's long-term interests.[9]

It may well have been that so volatile and emotional a man as Khrushchev had seized upon a rare opportunity to heap public scorn upon the leading nations of what he saw as the arrogant West, particularly the United States, which had so often held his own country in contempt and thwarted its interests and ambitions. Khrushchev might even have foreseen, by 1960 — as events far in the future were to demonstrate —

that the Soviet Union was too economically primitive and too hamstrung by an inefficient and oppressive political system to compete with, much less "bury," the West. Less than a year earlier, he had seen for himself the affluence, power, and advantages of the United States, and though he had blustered to Eisenhower about the "waste" of it all, who knows how he might privately have been impressed — and depressed — by what he had seen, in contrast to his own relatively backward homeland?

In any case, Khrushchev proceeded to wreck the summit he himself had helped bring about. In a shouting speech that caused de Gaulle, presiding, to tell him bluntly to tone it down, he denounced the United States and withdrew his invitation for Eisenhower to visit the Soviet Union. The president replied quietly that he had come to Paris for serious talks and hoped that the conferees now could engage in such discussion. But it was not to be; Khrushchev's graphic reply was to walk out, with the Soviet delegation dutifully following.

To Eisenhower, the imposing de Gaulle — not always an intimate or even an admirer of the World War II general or the later president — privately declared moving allegiance: "Whatever happens, I want you to know that I am with you to the end."

Thus passed the best hope and opportunity, until then, for a comprehensive test-ban treaty as the centerpiece of disarmament between hostile superpowers. Finished, too, was any possibility of achieving what had become one of Dwight Eisenhower's most cherished goals — for there would be no chance in his remaining eight months in office for so significant an agreement as the Paris summit had seemed to promise. The nuclear arms race and the Cold War, the vast expenditures to sustain both, with tensions only occasionally lessened and never removed, would continue for nearly thirty years, through seven more administrations, into the 1980s.

The Eisenhower administration itself, for practical purposes, had come to an end on a sad, even something of an Aristotelian, note. The 1960 campaign, Nixon's defeat, economic and diplomatic conflict with Castro's Cuba, more budget battles — all had yet to unfold. But shortly after Khrushchev shattered the Paris summit, the president said candidly and correctly to one of his scientific advisers that because of "the stupid U-2 mess . . . he saw nothing worthwhile left for him to do . . . until the end of his presidency."[10]

That prospect was all the more depressing in that Eisenhower must have known, and conceded to himself, that though Khrushchev had broken up the summit, the Soviet leader was not alone responsible for "the stupid U-2 mess." Whatever Khrushchev's motives and lack of control, Eisenhower had authorized that last mission over the Soviet Union, knowing its dangers, aware of its possible consequences, risking the crowning success that such a commanding man as Dwight Eisenhower must have wished for his epitaph. He had given Khrushchev the opportunity that the Soviet leader had seized upon, however unwisely, and Eisenhower's presidency had ended in disaster because of his own characteristic but needless gesture of self-assurance and pride in his and his country's prowess.

Ten

The collapse of the Paris summit in May 1959 did not, of course, literally mark the end of the Eisenhower administration, which still had seven months to go. The world was generally quiet and the administration mostly on hold in that interim, with the spectacular Nixon-Kennedy campaign and election of 1960 the most memorable events of the period. At least two notable additions, however, were made to the Eisenhower record.

The most celebrated, at the time, was a triumphal world tour the president undertook as his second term neared its end. His reception everywhere was tumultuous; the man of peace was welcomed with cheers and crowds all across Europe and Asia. People lined the roads as his limousine passed, and the world's press recorded every step and every word (none of which were of lasting importance). No former president had had the means (*Air Force One*) and the reason (global U.S. involvement) to make such a tour.

The trip left little doubt that Eisenhower himself had become the most popular, well-loved, and respected of the world's leaders — the disastrous consequences of the failed Paris summit not being as well understood in the immediate aftermath of Khrushchev's tantrums as they are nearly a half-century later. But there was little doubt, either, that the roaring welcome being extended to America's president was mostly personal — that while American power was respected and American policies and actions often were hailed, a divided and fearful world did not always love the American colossus itself, as that same world loved Dwight Eisenhower.

Less noticed at the time but of growing significance in the years since was Eisenhower's farewell address. Some inaugural speeches have become famous — Roosevelt's in 1933, for example, John Kennedy's in 1960. Eisenhower's two inaugurals are seldom remembered, and for good reason, but he shares with George Washington the distinction of having his last presidential words, rather than his first, enshrined in memory and lore.

In 1958, White House speechwriter Malcolm Moos gave the president a book of presidential speeches that included

Washington's farewell, in which the first president warned the nation to avoid "entangling alliances." The warning caught Eisenhower's eye, though it was far too early for him to begin thinking about a farewell. His last years in office, however, encompassed a long, almost endless battle against Democrats, some in his own administration, and the press, all of whom wanted to increase defense spending and build more weapons in the mistaken belief that the Soviet Union had forged ahead of the United States in military power.

Always careful to preserve U.S. economic as well as military strength, Eisenhower stood fast against these demands; he was bolstered in part by intelligence obtained from the high-flying, secret U-2 aircraft, but also by his own firm and experienced conviction that for deterrence "enough is enough," and that the United States already had more than enough to cope with, even overwhelm, the Soviet Union. But the president was profoundly disheartened by the forces clamoring for more, always more, defense spending.

Then, in late 1960, Moos and another writer, Ralph Williams, presented him with a memo detailing that the top hundred defense contractors employed 1,400 retired military officers, including 261 generals and admirals. "For the first time in its history," the two writers concluded, "the United States has a permanent war-based industry."

Their memo became the basic theme of the "great, sweeping document" that Norman Cousins, the editor of *Saturday Review*, had suggested Eisenhower prepare as a farewell. Moos completed a speech draft in December 1960; Eisenhower and his brother, Milton, edited it, including (at the suggestion of the White House science adviser, James Killian) shortening Moos's warning against a "military-industrial-scientific complex" to the phrase that would become famous: a "military-industrial complex."

Three days before John Kennedy was to be sworn in, Eisenhower spoke to the nation on the night of January 17, 1961. Americans, he warned, "face a hostile ideology, global in scope, atheistic in character, ruthless in purpose, and insidious in method." The danger threatened to be of "infinite duration" and, as a result, "we can no longer risk emergency improvisation of national defense; we have been compelled to create a permanent armaments industry of vast proportions."

Owing to this new combination of a military establishment and an arms industry exerting influence everywhere in government, the president continued in his solemn midwestern tones, "We must guard against the acquisition of unwarranted influence, whether sought or unsought, by the military-industrial complex. The potential for the disastrous rise of misplaced power exists and will persist."

The world paid little heed at the time; Kennedy's ringing inaugural address soon swamped Eisenhower's farewell — which had not been in any case a major theme of his time in office. Years later, President Nixon could even declare the "military-industrial complex" only a "straw-man issue," as he prepared to raise defense spending. But in the sixties and as Vietnam became a national horror, the import of Eisenhower's last words had lasted, grown, and echoed, not only in the United States but throughout the world. The old soldier turned father figure had done his duty again, at last warning the family that he had guarded so well, for so many years, that there was a danger within as well as a threat without.

In the years since he spoke, that internal danger has not always been credited or avoided, but because of President Eisenhower, Americans cannot say they weren't warned — and by one whose experience was too weighty to be ignored.

The Eisenhower administration, it's generally conceded, was largely successful in its foreign policy efforts. In a speech in Boston in 1962, the former president himself staked out a strong claim for its accomplishments:

> In those eight years we lost no inch of ground to tyranny. We witnessed no abdication of international respect. . . . [N]o walls were built.[1] No threatening foreign bases were established. One war was ended and incipient wars were blocked.

Yes, but . . . Eisenhower's personal inability to refuse that last, fatal U-2 mission was disastrous to the disarmament he by then wanted above all; nor has the world since achieved a comprehensive nuclear test-ban treaty. His major peace initiatives — "Atoms for Peace" and "Open Skies" — were admirable, world-pleasing gestures with little practical Cold War effect. He planted the seeds — at least tilled the ground — that later sprouted into the Bay of Pigs and the Vietnam War. He presided over and encouraged infamy in Iran and outrage in Guatemala.

Neither the president nor his greatest admirers have claimed for him any great record of success in domestic affairs, which was not his preferred operational area anyway. They can cite the Eisenhower interstate highway system, NASA, the Saint Lawrence Seaway, statehood for Hawaii (he opposed it for Alaska), and the first civil rights bill (albeit a weak one) in modern times, though he did little to achieve it.

On the other hand . . . Eisenhower's refusal to support the Supreme Court's historic *Brown* decision outlawing school segregation was perhaps his worst failure, one not altogether redeemed by his belated but firm enforcement of the ruling at Little Rock in 1957. His "strategy" against the tawdry charges of McCarthyism was at best slow and costly, though ultimately effective — but at worst, as many believe, less a strategy than a reluctance to engage. His arm's-length treatment of Richard Nixon and his myopic economic policy in 1959 were elements in the vice president's defeat in 1960, against Eisenhower's own and his party's interests.

Beyond political activity, Eisenhower also was a man whose personal tastes and preferences fitted all too well into the staid and conventional atmosphere of America in the fifties, and unfortunately did nothing to uplift or enlighten it. His preferred reading was Western novels. His painting was strictly a hobby, with no concern for art. He objected to a Picasso hanging in Gabriel Hauge's White House office, disliked classical music, and his son John conceded that the president's tastes were "strictly cornball." He spent much time at golf and bridge, usually in the company of the same group of wealthy businessmen, "achievers" like himself whom he admired and from whom he accepted expensive gifts that might well make a president today the target of a special prosecutor. Even so admiring an observer as William Ewald wrote that Eisenhower always got someone else to do the dirty work — a confirmation of Beetle Smith's "prat boy" recollection.[2]

Eisenhower also had a tart streak amounting sometimes to a lack of graciousness. The father figure in the White House could be privately acerbic and condescending even about men who had furthered his own career — FDR, for instance, had not needed to be so "indiscreet and crazy" at Yalta, Harry Truman was a "congenital liar," and it was a question whether even the Republican Thomas E. Dewey, twice a presidential candidate, four times governor of New York, one of Eisenhower's principle sponsors in 1952, had "matured" enough by 1956 to be again nominated for president.

Most Democrats were impossible — "men whom I have about as much political affinity for as a bull in a pen." Speaker Sam Rayburn would "doublecross you"; Senate Majority Leader Lyndon Johnson was a "phony"; and Averell Harriman a "nincompoop . . . a Park Avenue Truman." Even Republican colleagues were not immune: "Damn it, how in hell did a man as shallow as Charlie Wilson ever get to be head of General Motors?"[3]

One early morning in 1962, the phone woke me from a sound sleep in the St. Francis Hotel in San Francisco. I answered grudgingly and recognized the voice of my colleague and competitor, Earl Mazo of the *New York Herald-Tribune.*

"Get out to the airport quick, Wicker. I've got us on Eisenhower's plane."

Eisenhower? He was two years out of the White House, but his name still aroused — more sharply than had the insistent phone — my reporter's instinct.

"Don't go all the way to the public terminal. They're parked in the small plane area."

With no more information than that, in a few minutes I had packed my travel-light bag, settled my bill, and was in a cab for the airport. I had been traveling around the country writing about that year's important state and congressional elections, as national political reporter for the *New York Times*. The day before, I'd been covering Edmund G. "Pat" Brown, the genial incumbent governor of Californa, who was being challenged by Richard M. Nixon. Eisenhower, I knew, had been in the state to speak for his former vice president.

Having written a book about Nixon, Mazo had something of an "in" with him, which I supposed was why he'd been able to get himself a place on the Eisenhower plane. He'd gotten me a place, too, because Earl Mazo was always ready to help a younger colleague.

He was waiting for me by the steps of a small plane, and we hurried aboard.

Facing backward at a small table was Kevin McCann, whom I knew vaguely as a former presidential speechwriter. Facing forward across the same table, in the choice seat, was the great man himself. I had never met him, but "Ike" was for me, as for most Americans of the time, not only a familiar but a legendary figure — the victor of World War II, the president who had run the country for eight years, kept us out of war with the Russians, and still was the most popular man in an America that had not yet fallen in love with John F. Kennedy.

In Washington, I once had waited in a long line to get into one of Eisenhower's crowded news conferences; then, in an agony of rookie embarrassment, risen to ask a single question, which he'd answered affably, with no suggestion that he was talking to an impostor among familiar veterans.

That day on the plane, Mazo introduced me; Eisenhower shook my hand and went back immediately to chatting with McCann. Almost before I could seat myself across the aisle, the plane was moving out for takeoff. Thus began an unexpected week of close company with one of the most engaging men I have ever met.

★ ★ ★

The little plane would land at a small airport in a state like Idaho or Montana; a rally would be in progress for some Republican hopeful, occasionally an incumbent; the Eisenhower name would have brought out a substantial crowd; and the former president would emerge for a few brief, unfailingly partisan remarks — usually well informed by a McCann briefing just before the wheels touched down. Mazo and I would bounce out, too, ask a few questions, take notes, and follow Eisenhower and McCann back aboard for a quick takeoff — and on to the next stop, virtually identical with the last.

I filed a story every night, but so fleeting is political prominence that Eisenhower, no matter how welcome in South Dakota, was old news to the *Times*. Besides, he was not saying much, other than "elect this fine Republican for the good of your country." My stories usually wound up as what the *Times*, in its majesty, calls an "M-head" — maybe two paragraphs at the bottom of a column of more sensational stuff, with an unobtrusive headline: "Ike Backs GOP in Nebraska."

I don't remember the issues, or if there were any. What I do remember vividly is that when we were all airborne and relaxing again, only four of us in that tight little cabin, Dwight Eisenhower — merely sitting there chatting, occasionally grinning the famous grin, tossing back a handful of salted peanuts, his face effortlessly registering pleasure or inquiry or perplexity or regret or interest, whatever he was feeling — dominated every minute of the flight.

I had never supported him politically, but I was totally taken with him as a person. Not once did he make me feel uncomfortable to be in the presence of someone imposing — though he *was* imposing. I did not detect an impressive intellect behind his good humor and easy manner, but intellect had never been Eisenhower's greatest weapon (though he clearly was an intelligent man, and so keen an observer as George Kennan said after one meeting about foreign policy: "In summarizing the group's conclusions, President Eisenhower showed his intellectual ascendancy over every man in the room").[4]

I did see almost at once, however, what I think had made him a loved and respected father figure to so many Americans of the fifties. Ike was *somebody*. He was a presence — special, not ordinary. The crowds felt it when he emerged from the plane to speak.

Mazo and I felt it when we all climbed back inside — a magnetic quality, a center round which to gather. Even at close quarters, it was possible to turn your eyes away from Eisenhower — but you *knew* he was there anyway.

Once, when the likeable Gerald Ford was president, he held a White House reception for all former Republican national chairmen. William E. Miller remarked, on that occasion, to Meade Alcorn: "With Ford, you won't know he's in the room until you see him. With Ike, you always knew he was in the room even before you saw him."[5]

Eisenhower's obvious gravitas was unconcealed, however, by his magnetism or his usual good humor. His manner suggested always that here was someone to be depended upon, who could handle it — whatever it was — with a confidence that reenforced competence. Accustomed to ultimate decision, he conveyed security in his right to decide. Ample testimony exists that Eisenhower as general and president always was willing to listen, to hear, and even sometimes heed dissent. The incomparable press secretary Jim Hagerty thought Eisenhower's greatest achievement was in "getting people to compromise divergent views without anyone's sur-render of principle."[6] But just for that reason, it was clear that he should not be crossed idly or for no good reason.

No wonder, I thought many a time on that long flight east, that Dwight Eisen-hower could command men in war and lead them in peace. After we landed for the last time, at Gettysburg near the Eisen-hower farm, I never spent another personal moment with him, but forty years later, to me, Ike is still a commanding presence.

In putting together this book, I have tried not to let that well-remembered pres-ence influence my judgment or conclu-sions — just as I have been aware, in writing about Dulles, Hagerty, Nixon, Sherman Adams, and the rest of Eisen-hower's men, that with his personal mag-netism and his aura of competence and command, he must have had much the same effect on them as, on that compan-ionable flight, he had on me.

It could have been no small matter to work for and with such a man — to feel oneself carried with him on what could only have seemed, in his company and with his history, a mission. Indeed, the memoirs of his colleagues are replete with the sense of awe, the dedication with which they served him — perhaps more tangible even than any obligation they felt to their country.

For my part, from memory and research, I believe that Dwight D. Eisenhower was a great man — but not quite a great president. His opportunity — born of his presence, his experience, his competence, the trust placed in him, and the great world schism he inherited — was so immeasurable that perhaps no man, not even he, could have realized it.

Eisenhower's opportunity was different, too, from those the greatest presidents had faced: the Depression and World War II in Franklin Roosevelt's case, the Civil War in Lincoln's, the establishment of a nation in Washington's. All were severe challenges, of course, but all were opportunities for greatness, too. Eisenhower, facing his own challenge, repeatedly prevented war — but lacked the ultimate greatness to make peace; the worst did not happen in his time, but neither did the best. When he left office, in fact, the world was as divided and hostile, in some ways more so than when he was elected.

Eisenhower enforced the law in Little Rock, but never found it within himself to speak for equality of the races; he flattened Joe McCarthy with executive privilege, but impressed on Americans no moral outrage at McCarthy's sins against decency; he ended one war and blocked others, but Guatemalans paid in blood and oppression for an ideology as ruthless in purpose as any foreign creed.

It seems to me idle to try to identify what enabled a New York patrician, a midwestern railroad lawyer, a landed Virginia gentleman, to rise to greatness in meeting their different challenges. And it's just as useless to wonder why Eisenhower — clearly a great man while suffering with grace and dignity Khrushchev's fulminations in Paris — was less than a great president in sending off that unneeded U-2 flight that shattered so many possibilities.

Perhaps greatness is only in the eye of the beholder, and anyway, greatness in office surely requires more than greatness of self, since the latter may be found in countless lives obscure and famous — but the former is rare and indefinable, not to be predicted, for which there can be no experience. If Eisenhower reached greatness when he quelled panic after *Sputnik* and rejected gunboat diplomacy at Suez, it was as the man of character and steady vision that he had always been, rather than as a president of mysterious inspiration.

We seldom have need of a great president, after all, but we can never do without good men, in or out of office. Dwight Eisenhower was a good man, at times a great man, and it seems unnecessary to try to make him out a great president, too. He was elected to do a job he and the nation were confident he could handle, and he handled it well, perhaps better than anyone else could have. Americans will be fortunate if they can accord their future presidents trust and belief equal to that of the millions who expressed it so often in the fifties, in the simple but eloquent phrase:

"I Like Ike."

Notes

Chapter One

1. James C. Hagerty, *The Diary of James C. Hagerty: Eisenhower in Mid-Course, 1954–1955*, ed. Robert H. Ferrell (Bloomington, Ind.: Indiana University Press, 1983), 106. Unfortunately, Hagerty kept his entertaining and informative diary only for a brief period in Eisenhower's first term. Quotes from it are Hagerty's paraphrases, entered from memory after the day's work, but Hagerty was an able and experienced reporter who probably got the gist correctly.
2. Ibid., 48.
3. Ibid., 177. President Eisenhower told this strange story to Gov. Frank Lausche of Ohio in Hagerty's presence in 1955.
4. Robert Divine, *Eisenhower and the Cold War* (New York: Oxford University Press, 1981), 4.

5. Derived from a song of the same name by Irving Berlin, the second stanza of which concluded "Why even Harry Truman says 'I like Ike.' "

6. Stephen Ambrose, *Eisenhower: Soldier and President* (New York: Simon & Schuster Touchstone, 1991), 208.

7. Hagerty, *Diary*, 7.

8. Herbert Brownell with John P. Burke, *Advising Ike* (Lawrence, Kans.: University Press of Kansas, 1993), 99.

9. William Bragg Ewald, Jr., *Eisenhower the President: Crucial Days, 1951–1960* (Englewood Cliffs, N.J.: Prentice-Hall, 1981), 39.

10. Ibid., 31.

11. This device allowed several Eisenhower delegations from disputed states to be seated, instead of Taft delegations.

12. Brownell, *Advising Ike*, 126–29; Ambrose, *Eisenhower: Soldier and Patriot*, 285.

13. After Eisenhower won the election, Truman offered the president-elect the use of a government plane "if you still desire to go to Korea" — further igniting a developing enmity.

Chapter Two

1. Quoted in Fred Greenstein, *The Hidden-Hand Presidency: Eisenhower as Leader* (New York: Basic Books, 1982), 6.
2. Brownell wrote in later years that the president-elect told General James Van Fleet of this decision. Van Fleet passed on the story to Brownell, who believes Eisenhower never considered the offensive schemes of President Syngman Rhee of South Korea or the Pentagon. Brownell, *Advising Ike*, 137–39.
3. Emmett J. Hughes, *The Ordeal of Power*, 252; Arthur Larson, *Eisenhower: The President Nobody Knew* (New York: Charles Scribner's Sons, 1968), 75.
4. This was not a reward for Warren's having switched his delegates to Eisenhower at the Chicago convention. Warren never did switch his delegates, for reasons not yet certain.
5. Brownell, *Advising Ike*, 133–36.
6. Dwight D. Eisenhower, *Mandate for Change* (New York: Doubleday & Co., 1963), 75, 83. This is the first volume of the president's memoirs.

7. Larson, *Eisenhower: The President Nobody Knew*, 10.
8. Hagerty, *Diary*, 187.
9. David Kaiser, *American Tragedy* (Cambridge: Harvard University Press, 2000), 34.
10. Divine, *Eisenhower and the Cold War*, 12–17.
11. Eisenhower, *Mandate for Change*, 95.

Chapter Three

1. Divine, *Eisenhower and the Cold War*, 29.
2. John Prados, *Presidents' Secret Wars* (Chicago: Ivan R. Dee, 1996), 115–16.
3. Hagerty, *Diary*, 15.
4. The complete statement is in *Public Papers of the President*, vol. 54, 382–83, a government publication for each president.
5. Eisenhower told Stephen Ambrose this in a personal interview years later. Nixon, who was present with Cutler, recalled the occasion differently. Nor do the president's remembered words comport with other evidences of his views at the time. His statement to

Ambrose may therefore have exaggerated the vehemence of his response. Ambrose, *Eisenhower: Soldier and President*, 363.
6. Hagerty, *Diary*, 69.
7. Ibid., 48.
8. Blanche Weisen Cooke, *The Declassified Eisenhower* (New York: Doubleday, 1981), 269.
9. The CIA had persuaded publisher Arthur Hays Sulzberger to recall the *Times*'s correspondent in Mexico, Sydney Gruson, an assiduous reporter who had learned too much of the truth about Castillo's "uprising."
10. Eisenhower, *Mandate for Change*, 427.
11. Hagerty, *Diary*, 79.

Chapter Four

1. Ambrose, *Eisenhower: Soldier and President*, 378.
2. Hagerty, *Diary*, 43.
3. Ambrose, *Eisenhower: Soldier and President*, 341.
4. Hagerty, *Diary*, 61.
5. Ewald, *Eisenhower the President*, 39.
6. Larson, *Eisenhower: The President Nobody Knew*, 124–26.

7. Brownell's account of a meeting with SACEUR in Paris early in 1952 is in *Advising Ike*, 93–99.
8. Ibid., 166, 176.
9. Associate Justice Felix Frankfurter, in an exceptionally ungracious statement, told a clerk that this was "the first indication I have ever had that there is a God." James T. Patterson, *Brown v. Board of Education: A Civil Rights Milestone and Its Troubled Legacy* (New York: Oxford University Press, 2001), 57.
10. Ewald, *Eisenhower the President*, 82.
11. Patterson, *Brown v. Board of Education*, 55.
12. Ibid., 63.
13. Ibid., 65.
14. Ibid., 70–71.
15. Hagerty, *Diary*, 53.
16. All quotations from Larson, *Eisenhower: The President Nobody Knew*, 124–28.
17. Ambrose, *Eisenhower, Soldier and President*, 542.
18. Earl Warren, *The Memoirs of Earl Warren* (Garden City, N.Y.: Doubleday, 1977).
19. Ewald, *Eisenhower the President*, 86.
20. Larson, *Eisenhower: The President Nobody Knew*, 84.

Chapter Five

1. These included more than sixty-five phone calls, nineteen meetings with army representatives, a request for a commission for Schine and for special assignments for him. He had had fifteen passes between November 10, 1953, and January 16, 1954. Most other inductees had had no more than three passes.
2. Though at a news conference in Denver on August 22, 1952, Eisenhower had called Marshall "a perfect example of patriotism and loyal servant of the United States."
3. Letter to Harry Bullis, in Ambrose, *Eisenhower: Soldier and President*, 317.
4. Greenstein, *The Hidden-Hand Presidency*.
5. Sherman Adams, *Firsthand Report: The Story of the Eisenhower Administration* (New York: Harper & Bros., 1961).
6. This account of that early relationship is based on chapters 7 and 8 of Athan Theoharis, *Chasing Spies* (Chicago: Ivan R. Dee, 2002).
7. That is, he claimed Fifth Amendment protection against the possibility of in-

criminating himself. Cold Warriors seldom failed to draw the most damaging conclusion from such a plea.

8. Arthur Herman, *Joseph McCarthy: Reexamining the Life and Legacy of America's Most Hated Senator* (New York: Free Press, 2000), 248–50.

9. Greenstein, *Hidden-Hand Presidency*, 185.

10. Hagerty, *Diary*, 19–20.

11. Greenstein, *Hidden-Hand Presidency*, 191.

12. An Eisenhower news conference usually was "on background," meaning his remarks had to be paraphrased rather than quoted verbatim.

13. Eisenhower had recommended John W. Davis, who in that same year, 1954, had defended school segregation in the case of *Brown v. Board of Education.*

14. Hagerty, *Diary*, 53; Ambrose, *Eisenhower: Soldier and President*, 365.

15. Greenstein, *Hidden-Hand Presidency*, 205.

16. Ibid., 205, 207.

17. Herman, *Joseph McCarthy*, 269.

18. Eisenhower's executive privilege doctrine stands to this day. Federal courts have made only limited exceptions to

permit noncongressional investigators, such as a court-appointed special prosecutor, to subpoena executive branch information, but only when the information can be shown to be necessary to a criminal investigation.

19. Herman, *Joseph McCarthy*, 262.
20. This account of the Welch-McCarthy exchange follows that of Arthur Herman in *Joseph McCarthy*, 275–76.

Chapter Six

1. Hagerty, *Diary*, 193.
2. Ambrose, *Eisenhower: Soldier and President*, 384.
3. Later, when preparing his memoirs, Eisenhower had to be reminded, according to William Ewald, that Open Skies originally was Rockefeller's plan. See Ewald, *Eisenhower the President*, 235.
4. Ambrose, *Eisenhower: Soldier and President*, 392.
5. Charles E. Bohlen, *Witness to History* (New York: W. W. Norton, 1973), 384.
6. Ambrose, *Eisenhower: Soldier and President*, 396.
7. Hagerty, *Diary*, 236–37.

8. Arthur Burns told me that Eisenhower once speculated that Harry F. Byrd, Sr., the Democratic boss of Virginia, might be persuaded to run for president on the Republican ticket.
9. Eisenhower even persuaded Republican Party chairman Len Hall to suggest to Nixon that the Roman Catholic governor of Ohio, Frank Lausche, might be a good vice presidential candidate, though Lausche was a Democrat. When Hall told this to Nixon, he "never saw a scowl come so fast over a man's face."
10. Ambrose, *Eisenhower: Soldier and President*, 427.
11. Ibid., 431.

Chapter Seven

1. I have a strong memory of the impressive Russell as I saw him from the Senate press gallery, red-faced and raising clenched fists, thundering that the bill was "about schools!" rather than voting rights.
2. Two future Democratic presidents voted for this final compromise for opposite reasons — John F. Kennedy

of Massachusetts, to attract southern support for his national campaign, and Lyndon B. Johnson of Texas to persuade northerners that he was not a prisoner of a southern background.

3. Eisenhower's diary entry was dictated to Ann Whitman, his secretary. Brownell, *Advising Ike*, 206–10.

4. Ibid., 211–13. Brownell thought that Eisenhower's attitude toward Faubus, after their Newport meeting, was that of a "military commander in chief, dealing with . . . a subordinate who had let him down in the midst of battle."

5. As a Neiman Fellow at Harvard in 1957, I remember some professors gathering on a bridge over the Charles River and applauding *Sputnik*'s highly visible nighttime passage across the sky.

6. A probably apocryphal story had it that a Maryland politician had called on the air force to shoot down *Sputnik* if it overflew Baltimore.

7. So William Ewald theorized in *Eisenhower the President*.

8. For the rest of his life, much to his annoyance, Eisenhower suffered such

minor speech impediments as reversing syllables in a long word. Few listeners ever noticed.

9. Ewald, *Eisenhower the President*, 262.

Chapter Eight

1. Dwight Eisenhower, *Waging Peace* (New York: Doubleday & Co., 1976), 270. This is the second volume of Eisenhower's memoirs.

2. Townsend Hoopes, *The Devil and John Foster Dulles* (Boston: Little, Brown and Co., 1973), 435.

3. Ultimately, the equivalent of a division was landed in Lebanon. It was backed by two more divisions on alert in Germany.

4. So did a young editorial writer named Wicker, who threatened fruitlessly to resign from the Winston-Salem, N.C., *Journal* when wiser heads refused to publish his article critical of the intervention.

5. So he told Herbert Klein, his press secretary, who in a later interview repeated the remark to me.

6. All the quotations in this and the previous paragraph are from Ewald,

Eisenhower the President, 266, 270.

7. Ambrose, *Eisenhower: Soldier and President,* 492.
8. Ibid., 489.
9. On a train between Washington and New York, Khrushchev shook hands with Roger Mudd, Charles McDowell, and me, saying affably, *"Mir y druzhba."* We soon were told that these words meant "peace and friendship" in Russian, and that he was greeting other reporters with the same phrase.
10. Anderson was a Democrat, whom Eisenhower admired and urged to run for vice president in 1956 and for president in 1960 on the Republican ticket. In 1987, Anderson pled guilty to tax evasion and illegal banking charges.
11. After the 1960 election, Nixon went to visit William McChesney Martin, then the chairman of the Federal Reserve Board, and told Martin to his face that his tight-money policy had been largely responsible for Nixon's and the Republican Party's narrow defeat.
12. Ewald, *Eisenhower the President,* 310.

Chapter Nine

1. True to form, Eisenhower had hoped Nixon would choose Treasury Secretary Robert Anderson to run for the vice presidency.
2. Related by Moos in a private conversation.
3. Ewald, *Eisenhower the President*, 312–13.
4. An idea proposed by Senator Albert Gore of Tennessee, a member of the Geneva delegation and the father of the Democrats' presidential candidate in 2000.
5. McGeorge Bundy, John Kennedy's national security adviser, put the number at 18,000 at the end of the fifties, in *Danger and Surivival: Choices About the Bomb in the First Fifty Years* (New York: Random House, 1988).
6. In 1962, the U-2 was similarly to tip off the Kennedy administration to the installation of Soviet missiles in Cuba.
7. As President Kennedy conceded in 1961, after having reaped political benefit from a charge he and other Democrats often had made in the 1960 campaign.

8. Eisenhower told his secretary, Ann Whitman, about the possibility of his resignation, and she recorded the remark in her diary.

9. De Gaulle, owing to wartime difficulties, could hardly be called an "old friend."

10. George Kistiakowsky, *A Scientist at the White House* (Cambridge: Harvard University Press, 1976), 375.

Chapter Ten

1. A reference to the Berlin Wall, built by the Soviets in 1961, and a jab at the Kennedy administration.

2. Ewald, *Eisenhower the President*. On Hauge's Picasso and the "cornball" remark, see p. 170. The "dirty work" observation is on p. 262.

3. Hagerty, *Diary*: on Dewey, 240; Democrats, 30. Ewald, *Eisenhower the President*: on FDR, 26; LBJ, 27; Rayburn, 28; Truman, 32; Wilson, 189–92. Tom Wicker, *One of Us* (New York: Random House, 1991): on Harriman, 198.

4. Ewald, *Eisenhower the President*, 169.

5. Ibid., 73.

6. Ibid., 72.

Milestones

1890   Dwight D. Eisenhower born in Denison, Texas, on October 14. Family moves to Abilene, Kansas, the following year.

1911   Takes service exam and wins admission to West Point.

1915   Graduates in "the class the stars fell on" and is commissioned.

1916   Marries Mamie Doud in Denver on July 1.

1921   Their firstborn son, Doud Dwight, dies aged three, on January 2.

1922   Sent to 20th Infantry Brigade in Panama Canal Zone; comes under influence of the commanding general, Fox Connor.

1925   Connor arranges for Eisenhower to go to Army Command and General Staff School, from which he graduates the next year, first in his class.

1927   General John J. Pershing sends Eisenhower to Army War College.

1929   Returns to Washington as aide to General Douglas MacArthur.

1935 Accompanies MacArthur to Philippines as chief of staff.

1939 World War II begins in September in Europe. Eisenhower returns to United States.

1941 Promoted colonel; assigned as chief of staff to Third Army; gains public notice in Louisiana maneuvers. Promoted brigadier general; summoned to War Department after Japanese attack Pearl Harbor in December.

1942 Promoted major general; assigned by General George Marshall to head War Plans Division, then sent to London to command European Theater of Operations. Roosevelt and Churchill order Torch (invasion of North Africa) instead of Sledgehammer (cross-Channel invasion). Eisenhower named to command Torch.

1943 Promoted to four-star general; named to command Overlord (new name for cross-Channel invasion).

1944 Overlord landings succeed on D day, June 6. Last German offensive briefly halts Allies in "Battle of the Bulge."

1945 Allies cross Rhine on March 17. Roosevelt dies April 12; Truman succeeds. Germans surrender on

May 7. First atomic bomb is dropped on Hiroshima, in Japan, August 6. Pacific war ends with Japanese surrender on August 14. Truman appoints Eisenhower army chief of staff.

1948 Turns down offers from both parties to run for president. Publishes *Crusade in Europe*. Becomes president of Columbia University. Truman is reelected in November.

1950 Korean War begins. Eisenhower appointed SACEUR (supreme allied commander, Europe) to organize NATO army.

1952 Wins New Hampshire primary as write-in candidate; becomes announced candidate; defeats Taft at Republican National Convention; chooses Richard Nixon as running mate; wins presidency on November 4 with 442 electoral votes, including those from five states of the formerly "Solid South."

1953 Inaugurated on January 20. Joseph Stalin dies on March 8. Korean Armistice signed July 27. Earl Warren appointed chief justice. Senator Joseph R. McCarthy begins investigation of U.S. Army. Government of

Iran overthrown by CIA in "secret war."

1954 John Foster Dulles labels new defense policy "massive resistance." Arbenz government overthrown in Guatemala. J. Robert Oppenheimer's security clearance revoked. Chief Justice Warren announces unanimous Supreme Court decision ending school segregation. Eisenhower decides against U.S. intervention in French war in Indo-China. Dienbienphu falls. Geneva conference divides Indo-China into North and South Vietnam. Army-McCarthy hearings begin on April 22. Executive privilege doctrine disclosed May 7. GOP loses control of Congress in November elections. Senate votes 67–22 to "condemn McCarthy" on December 2.

1955 War threatens, is avoided, over Quemoy, Matsu, and Formosa. Geneva summit hears "Open Skies" proposal; results only in "spirit of Geneva." Eisenhower suffers coronary thrombosis in Denver September 20.

1956 Announces in February that he'll run again. Opposes British, French, Israelis in November crisis in Middle East. Soviet armed force quells Hungarian uprising. Eisenhower-Nixon ticket wins landslide reelection.

1957   First civil rights bill of modern times approved. *Brown* decision enforced at Little Rock, Arkansas. Soviets launch *Sputnik I* successfully. Recession begins.

1958   Orders a successful intervention in Lebanon. Economy recovers.

1959   Castro takes over Cuba on January 1. Khrushchev forces Berlin crisis. John Foster Dulles dies. New recession begins. Khrushchev visits United States.

1960   Authorizes last U-2 flight on eve of Paris summit. Khrushchev breaks up summit after spy plane shot down over Russia. Eisenhower makes triumphal world tour. Nixon-Lodge ticket defeated by Kennedy-Johnson.

1961   Leaves office on January 20.

1969   Dies on March 28.

Selected Bibliography

Adams, Sherman. *Firsthand Report: The Story of the Eisenhower Administration.* New York: Harper and Row, 1961.

Ambrose, Stephen. *Eisenhower: Soldier and President.* New York: Simon & Schuster Touchstone, 1991.

Bohlen, Charles. *Witness to History.* New York: W. W. Norton, 1973.

Brownell, Herbert, with John P. Burke. *Advising Ike.* Lawrence, Kans.: University Press of Kansas, 1993.

Bundy, McGeorge. *Danger and Survival.* New York: Vintage, 1990.

Cook, Blanche W. *The Declassified Eisenhower.* Garden City, N.Y.: Doubleday & Co., 1981.

Divine, Robert. *Eisenhower and the Cold War.* New York: Oxford University Press, 1981.

Eisenhower, Dwight D. *Mandate for Change* and *Waging Peace*, vols. 1 and 2 of the president's memoirs. Garden City, N.Y.: Doubleday & Co., 1963 and 1974.

Ewald, William. *Eisenhower the President;*

Crucial Days: 1953–1960. Englewood Cliffs, N.J.: Prentice-Hall, 1981.

Ferrell, Robert, ed. *The Diary of James Hagerty.* Bloomington, Ind.: Indiana University Press, 1983.

Greenstein, Fred. *Eisenhower, the Hidden-Hand Presidency.* New York: Basic Books, 1982.

Herman, Arthur. *Joseph McCarthy.* New York: The Free Press, 2000.

Hoopes, Townsend. *The Devil and John Foster Dulles.* New York: Little, Brown & Company, 1973.

Hughes, Emmet. *The Ordeal of Power.* New York: Atheneum, 1963.

Kaiser, David. *American Tragedy.* Cambridge, Mass.: Harvard University Press, 2000.

Kistiakowsky, George B., and Charles S. Maier. *A Scientist at the White House.* Cambridge, Mass.: Harvard University Press, 1976.

Krock, Arthur. *Memoirs: Sixty Years on the Firing Line.* New York: Funk & Wagnalls, 1968.

Larson, Arthur. *Eisenhower: The President Nobody Knew.* New York: Charles Scribner's Sons, 1968.

Patterson, James. *Brown v. Board of Education: A Civil Rights Milestone.* New York: Oxford University Press, 2001.

Pickett, William B. *Eisenhower Decides to Run*. Chicago: Ivan R. Dee, 2000.

Prados, John. *Presidents' Secret Wars*. Chicago: Ivan R. Dee, 1996.

Theoharis, Athan. *Chasing Spies*. Chicago: Ivan R. Dee, 2002.

Warren, Earl. *The Memoirs of Earl Warren*. Garden City, N.Y.: Doubleday & Co., 1977.

About the Author

For over thirty years, Tom Wicker covered American politics at the *New York Times*, where he began writing the *Times*'s "In the Nation" column. He is the author of seventeen books, including *One of Us: Richard Nixon and the American Dream*, *JFK and LBJ*, and ten novels.

57